BIBLE STUDY

Lessons:

....

Weekly Plans for Church Leaders

3 Months of Lessons Complete With Biblical Research, Stories & Discussion

VOLUME 1

JOHN W. WARNER

WORKBOOK

Praise for "Prepared Bible Study Lessons"

"We used this book for a Sunday school lesson for adults. We loved this study; it is very thought provoking and encouraged discussion. We have learned so many things from the in-depth research that was put into this Bible study. It is by far the best lesson we have used to date. I am so ready for the future volumes to be published.

- Mayetta Holland

"This book is well-researched, thought-provoking and it's a hands-on and interactive way of preparing bible study lessons. Overall, the book is structured, Spiritual and it would make a great gift."

- Bryon Tyler

"This is a nifty book! If you endeavor to teach Sunday school lessons or simply need content for small bible study groups, this is an indispensable resource. Lots of topical material to draw from as well as interesting historical asides. Easy to read and easy to use. All in all, an excellent guide."

- Michael S. Sanders

"These lessons would be very easy for anyone to use. They are informative, with well researched additional details that make them interesting even to those familiar with the Biblical texts. The use of several different scripture translations gives added clarity. I like how each lesson begins and ends with prayer. I would highly recommend this book to anyone teaching a Sunday School class."

- Jackie L

"Our class enjoyed the discussion questions, and the real-life applications of the lessons."
- Pat Johnson

Thank you for reading this book and leaving an honest review

Dedication

This book is dedicated to my wife of 60 years, my proofreader, my best friend, Judy Warner.

Acknowledgements

Thanks to the members of the Koinonia Sunday School Class of the First United Methodist Church in Pampa, Texas, whose discussion added depth to these lessons.

Table of Contents

INTRODUCTION

I'm a practicing attorney for over 50 years. I have taught a youth and adult Sunday School Class in the First United Methodist Church in Pampa, Texas, for 50 years. I enjoy the process of researching and providing "evidence" of God. Some of these lessons took a few hours or days to prepare. I have studied the Shroud of Turin for over 30 years. I have presented thousands of programs to churches, Sunday School classes, civic clubs, and other groups.

In 2020 our church discontinued Sunday School temporarily because of Covid-19. In order to feel more connected to our class, I developed a series of lessons that I presented online to our Sunday School class. We had virtual meetings for almost 6 months.

These lessons are reproduced for you here. These lessons should be used as resource materials rather than Lessons 1 through 13. They can be presented live or in a virtual setting online. Lessons 1, 2 and 3 are appropriate around Easter. The Ten Commandments should be presented on successive Sundays. The other lessons are not in any particular order.

Class members willing to read scriptures should be contacted in advance and assigned scriptures to read. This involves the class members and has them prepared to read immediately rather than having to look the scriptures up during class time. Having class members read scriptures or sing the music recommended helps them get involved and take ownership of the class.

The questions for class discussion during the lessons and the lessons are designed to be about 35-45 minutes long. One purpose of the lessons is to get class members to examine and think about their faith and then put their faith into action.

Each chapter can be used as a separate weekly lesson or sermon topic.

Email me at jww_pampa@yahoo.com for questions, comments, or programs for your church or civic group.

My prayer is that God may speak to your group through these lessons during your group experience.

STEP ONE – PICK A TIME & PLACE TO MEET WITH GOD

Before you jump into the actual workbook experiment, I want to share some practical tips I have learned over the years and how to have devotional time with God.

Whether you are doing this alone, with a partner or with a group – the key is to be consistent in your meeting with God.

Choose a time that you can be fully engaged and present with the word. I believe that God always gives us His best, so I want to respond by spending time with Him when I am alert and ready to receive.

Your meetings can take place at a church, in a home or a place that is peaceful without many distractions.

If you are doing this alone, pick a time each day or week to go through the lessons and make it a priority.

You can use a digital Bible app or a hard copy to research the scripture.

STEP TWO – COMMIT TO THE PROCESS

As you get into the word of God, make sure you take time to pray or ask to receive the information or purpose that God wants you to have with this material.

I've found that even the same words can have a unique impact on people depending on their circumstances. It is during my time with God, I bring my questions to Him. Curiosity and questions are all part of the scientific process of understanding how the material relates to our daily life and how to apply it.

When you do this with a group, it creates more engagement and discussion. Many different versions of the Bible were used to present this information, so you will also see the biblical references in the text.

STEP THREE – LISTEN AND WRITE

God speaks to us through the word. Sometimes we are so busy doing things, we miss what He is trying to share with us.

When we are fully engaged and asking questions, then it is equally important to write down the thoughts that come from doing the exercises or using the tools that you will learn here.

OTHER NOTES TO ENGAGE THE GROUP

If you are using this as a guide to lead a group, then you might ask different people to read the questions or share the stories used as an example.

Feel free to also include personal stories that might relate to the context or event.

All prayers and questions are in italics, so it's easy to see where the group leader can ask for reflection.

CHAPTER 1
JESUS' ARREST AND TRIAL

Prayer

Lord, today help us to listen, help us to learn and help us to live according to Your will. In Jesus' name. Amen.

The Garden of Gethsemane

Picture in your minds the Garden of Gethsemane in the First Century. It is on the Mount of Olives. It is night. There is a full moon. The garden is lit up almost as bright as day.

Rich people have gardens outside of the city limits of Jerusalem because space in Jerusalem is too limited for private gardens. In addition, there are ceremonial prohibitions which forbid the use of manure on the soil of Jerusalem because it is a sacred city.

I picture a lush garden with a fence around it and a locked gate. Thus, a rich man probably loaned Jesus a key so he could go to the garden and take his disciples with him when he wanted peace and quiet.

Judas would know that Jesus was likely to be there. He probably thought that would be the easiest place to make the arrest.

Upper Room

Jesus and His disciples had just finished eating the Feast of the Passover in the Upper Room. Jesus had just told Judas to go do what he was going to do. Jesus had confided to John that Judas was the one who would betray Him.

John 18:1-3 (Living New Testament) "1. After saying these things Jesus crossed the Kidron ravine with His disciples and entered a grove of olive trees. 2. Judas, the betrayer, knew this place, for Jesus had gone there many times with His disciples. 3. The chief priests and Pharisees had given Judas a squad of soldiers and police to accompany him. Now with blazing torches, lanterns, and weapons they arrived at the olive grove."

Kidron

What is the significance of crossing the Kidron ravine? Why would that detail be included in the Bible?

The Feast of the Passover or the Feast of Unleaven Bread was celebrated in Jerusalem in about April of our calendar each year during Jesus' life. The celebration lasted a week. Some say eight days. Mosiac law required all able-bodied men 13 years of age and older to attend if they were physically able and ceremonially clean.

Some authorities estimate that the population of Jerusalem in Jesus' time was as little as 25,000. They also estimate that as many as 256,000 lambs were offered as sacrifices during the Passover. With an average of 10 to 20 men per lamb, we are looking at over two million people who would have flocked to Jerusalem during the Passover.

Picture the temple as being located at the highest point in that area. The lambs were killed in the Temple courtyard. The priests lined up 10 deep. They had cups of gold or silver which were rounded on the bottom so they could not be put down. A priest would fill the cup as the lamb bled and hand it to another priest who would hand him an empty cup. They would pass the cup down to the last priest in line who would then sprinkle the blood on the alter.

Where did the blood go? Down a trough. Then they washed the blood with water down the Kidron ravine. My estimate is that each synagogue could kill as many as 600 lambs per hour or 6,000 in a 10-hour period. There were at least 480 synagogues in Jerusalem in Jesus' time.

Isn't it ironic that Jesus and his disciples had to cross a river of lambs' blood in order to get to the Garden of Gethsemane shortly before the Lamb of God shed his precious blood?

Sweat Blood

What did Jesus do in the Garden of Gethsemane?

The Bible tells us that he prayed so hard and so earnestly that he literally sweated blood.

This is a very rare condition known as hematidrosis (he mat ah drosis). It happens when we are under extreme mental or physical stress. Blood will usually oozes from the forehead, nails, navel and other skin surfaces. It sometimes results in tears of blood.

Squad

The Living New Testament says Judas had a "squad" of soldiers. The King James Version says it was a "band" of men. The Amplified Version and the Revised Standard Version say it was a "band" of soldiers. When I think of a "squad" or a "band," I think of a group of 25 to 50 or so. Our squadron at Texas A&M had 56 in it.

The New International Version said: "So Judas came to the grove guiding a detachment of soldiers and some officials from the chief priests and Pharisees." John 18:3. A "detachment" was a group of 300 to 600 soldiers.

The actual word used was "speira," which has three meanings. It was a Greek word for a "cohort." A cohort had 600 men. However, if it were a cohort of auxiliary soldiers, it had 1,000 men. The auxiliary cohort had 240 cavalry men and 760 infantry members. A third meaning, which was rarely used, meant a "maniple." That consisted of only 200 men. Now in addition to the speira, there were also temple police and Sanhedrin police. So, a force of over 200 and maybe more than 1,000 well-armed men with torches and lanterns came seeking Jesus.

Why did they have torches and lanterns when there was a full moon?

They expected Jesus to hide. They were expecting to look for Him in the nooks and crannies of the Garden of Gethsemane.

John 18:4 (LB) "Jesus fully realized all that was going to happen to Him."

Arrest

Let's try to picture the arrest.

John 18:5-8 (LB) "Stepping forward to meet them He asked, 'Whom are you looking for?' 'Jesus of Nazareth,' they replied. "I am He,' Jesus said. (Demonstrate how the soldiers fell back, lost their balance and fell down in the presence of Jesus.) 6. "And as He said it, they all fell backwards to the ground! 7. Once more He asked them, 'Whom are you searching for?' And again they replied, "Jesus of Nazareth.' 8. 'I told you I am He.'"

John is the only one of the Gospel writers who describes Jesus' arrest in this fashion. The other three proclaim that Judas betrayed Jesus with a kiss.

Jesus asked the soldiers to let his disciples go and they did. Peter, though badly outnumbered, drew his sword and cut off the right ear of Malchus, the high priest's servant. Jesus told him to put up his sword and healed the man's ear.

Thus, Jesus was arrested at night in the Garden of Gethsemane. But think about Peter's initial reaction and courage. He was one man with a sword against more than 200 heavily armed soldiers and police. To fight against those odds was suicide. But his initial reaction was to protect Jesus even at the cost of his own life. Jesus, though, rebuked him for his reaction.

Peter

Before we go on, let's think a little more about Peter. Remember Christ predicted:

John 13:38 (RSV) "Truly, truly I say to you, the cock will not crow, till you have denied me three times."

Luke 22:61 (RSV) "Before the cock crows today, you will deny me three times."

Mark 14:30 (KJV) "Verily I say unto thee, that this day, even in this night, before the cock crow twice, thou shall deny me thrice."

Matthew 26:34 (KJV) "Verily I say unto thee, that this night, before the cock crow, thou shalt deny me thrice."

What time of day are we talking about? I have always thought it happened about day break. I always pictured a rooster crowing. Some translations of the Bible even say so.

John 13:38 (Amplified New Testament) "Jesus answered, Will you lay down your life for Me? I assure you, most solemnly I tell you, before a rooster crows you will deny Me–completely disown Me–three times."

Luke 22:60 (LB) "But Peter said, 'Man, I don't know what you are talking about.' And as he said the words, a rooster crowed."

Remember that Jesus was arrested after dark. He was taken first to the castle of Annas and then to the castle of Caiaphas. Jesus "trial" has not even started. It is the middle of the night.

How or why would a rooster crow in the middle of the night?

Also, know that it is against the law to keep chickens in the Holy City. Just as the Jews did not want gardens in the Holy City because they would not put manure on Holy Ground, they did not want chickens defiling the Holy City either.

The Roman army had four watches during the night.
The first watch was from 6 p.m. to 9 p.m.
The second watch was from 9 p.m. to midnight.
The third watch was from midnight to 3 a.m.

At precisely 3 a.m., before the fourth watch, a bugle would sound. That was known as "cock crow." Thus, Jesus could well have been referring to the bugle "cock crow" rather than a rooster crowing. If you use the New International Version of the Bible, you will see this information in a footnote.

As I mentioned before, some translations specifically say "rooster." For example: Matthew 26:34 (Amplified Version) "Solemnly I declare to you, this very night before a single rooster crows you will deny and disown Me three times."

But compare: Mark 13:35-37 (New Revised Standard Version) "Keep awake–for you do not know when the master of the house will come, in the evening, or at midnight, or at cockcrow, or at dawn, or else he finds you asleep when he comes suddenly."

So sometime that evening before 3 a.m., Peter probably denied Our Lord three times.

Sixth Hour

It was probably about 6 a.m. when Pilate pronounced the death sentence.

John 19:14-16 (NIV) "It was the day of Preparation of Passover Week, about the sixth hour. 'Here is your king,' Pilate said to the Jews. 15 But they shouted, 'Take him away! Take him away! Crucify him! Crucify him!' 'Shall I crucify your king?' Pilate asked. 'We have no king but Caesar,' the chief priests answered. 16 Finally Pilate handed him over to them to be crucified."

Players

Let's think about who the players are in the trial of Jesus: Annas, Caiaphas, members of the Sanhedrin, Herod and Pontius Pilate.

Annas

Annas was the son of Seth. He was appointed the first High Priest of Judaea in 6 A.D. by the Roman Legate Quirinius. He served 10 years and was removed from office at the age of 36 by the Roman curator, Gratis. The high priest was supposed to serve for life. Thus, he remained a powerful political and social figure and was still referred to as the "high priest." After he was deposed, four or five of his sons bribed their way into a type of puppet High Priest as did his son-in-law Caiaphas. Annas maintained the actual power.

The Jews detested Annas. When the Romans came, the position of high priest often went to the highest bidder. It was a matter of corruption and bribery. The high priest closely cooperated with the Romans.

Annas was immensely wealthy. He made his money by selling doves and lambs as victims for the sacrifice in the Court of the Gentiles. If a Jew brought in a lamb or doves to sacrifice, they had to be perfect. An inspector would examine them and find some flaw. Then the worshiper would have to buy a sacrifice from one of the traders in the Temple. Annas charged 15 times more for two doves than what they sold for outside the Temple. That prompted Jesus to overturn their tables and call them thieves and robbers.

John 18:13 (LNT) "First they took Him to Annas, the father-in-law of Caiaphas, the High Priest that year."

Jesus was first taken before Annas because his castle was closer. Annas questioned Jesus about his disciples and his teaching and sent him to Caiaphas.

Caiaphas (pronounced "kia fuss")

Joseph Caiaphas was married to Annas' daughter. He was appointed High Priest by Valerius Gratus in A. D. 18 and kept the position until A.D. 36. He was the Jewish High Priest and the President of the Sanhedrin, The Jewish Supreme Court. He was the ring leader who organized the plot to kill Jesus. He was worried that if Jesus were allowed to continue, the people would believe him and the Romans would come and destroy the Jewish holy place and nation. He makes the political rationalization that it is better for one man (Jesus) to die than the whole nation to be destroyed.

John 18:14 (LNT) "Caiaphas was the one who told the other Jewish leaders, 'Better that one should die for all.'"

John 18:19-21 (LNT) "Inside, the High Priest (Caiaphas) began asking Jesus about His followers and what he had been teaching them. 20. Jesus replied, 'What I teach is widely known, for I have preached regularly in the synagogue and Temple; I have been heard by all the Jewish leaders and teach nothing in private that I have not said in public. 21. Why are you asking Me this question? Ask those who heard Me. You have some of them here. They know what I said.'"

Jesus knows the Jewish law. He knows that a prisoner may not be asked any question that might incriminate himself. Jesus does not have to testify against Himself. Caiaphas is breaking one of the rules of the Sanhedrin in asking this type of question of Jesus. Jesus was reminding Caiaphas of this.

Then, in the most critical part of the trial before the Sanhedrin, Caiaphas asks Jesus: "Are you the Messiah? Are you the Son of God?" At this point if Jesus says, "No," the whole "trial" falls apart. They would have been forced to let him go. He would be a free man. However, if Jesus answers, "Yes," then He is doomed to the cross. It may be this time that Jesus pauses to reflect before He answers. He knows full well what a truthful answer to that question will bring. This is the Achilles heel of Jesus. And, get this, under the rules of the Sanhedrin, Jesus is NOT required to testify against Himself.

Luke 22:70-71 (LNT) "They all shouted, 'Then you claim you are the Son of God?' And He replied, 'Yes, I am.' 71. 'What need do we have for other witnesses?' they shouted, 'for we ourselves have heard him say it.'"

Jesus replies, "I am." Then the whole place goes crazy. Caiaphas and others tear their clothes and denounce Jesus as being guilty of "blasphemy." They can now charge Jesus with sedition, a charge they know that Pilate will listen to. The Sanhedrin unanimously finds Jesus guilty and orders Jesus beaten, but it has no power to impose the death penalty. They spit on him and slap him in the face. Any semblance of justice or a court of law evaporates. Remember that the verdict was unanimous.

Sanhedrin

The Sanhedrin was the Jewish Supreme Court. Its 70-72 sages were Scribes, Pharisees and Sadducees.

The Scribes were wealthy upper class men who studied the law of Moses, taught it to the people and settled disputes involving questions of the law.

Pharisees were middle class businessmen, who meticulously adhered to their interpretation of the Torah. They had 613 laws which they religiously followed: 248 positive laws, one for every part of the body and 365 negative laws, one for every day of the year. They were popular with the people, and, as a result, they often controlled the decisions of the Sanhedrin because they were popular. They believed in the oral traditions and the written word. They believed in the resurrection and an afterlife. They were more concerned with religion than politics.

Jesus compared the Pharisees to a tomb. It was white on the outside but dead on the inside.

The Sadducees were a religious movement of the wealthy Jewish elite. They maintained the temple in Jerusalem. They had priestly responsibility. They collected taxes and led the army. The Sadduccees mediated domestic disputes and believed that the written Torah was the sole source of divine authority. Unlike the Pharisees, they believed in no afterlife or resurrection of the dead. They held the majority of the seats on the Sanhedrin. They were more concerned with politics than religion and were very accommodating to Rome.

Jesus called the Sadducees "sons of snakes." The Sadduccees probably suffered financial losses when Jesus chased the moneychangers out of the temple because they likely received a cut of the profits.

The Pharisees and Sadducees were the ruling class of Israel. They were the elders of the people. There were 12 tribes of Israel and six elders in each tribe. They were the representatives of the nation. Even today some Christian churches have elders who govern their churches.

It takes 23 members to form a quorum of the Sanhedrin for a trial such as Jesus'.

Luke 23:1 (LNT) "Then the entire Council took Jesus over to Pilate, the governor."

That sounds like they had 100 percent attendance.

The Sanhedrin regulations require that all criminal cases must be tried and completed during the day time. Jesus' trial took place at night. Only if the verdict were "not guilty" could a trial begin and end on the same day. That was so that feelings of mercy would have time to develop. Jesus was convicted in a few hours–all at night.

No decision of the Sanhedrin was valid unless they met in their own meeting place, which was known as the Hall of Hewn Stone. For Jesus' trial, they met in the homes of Annas and Caiaphas.

All evidence had to be guaranteed by two witnesses who were examined separately. False witness was punishable by death. The trial was supposed to begin with laying before the court all of the evidence for the innocence of the accused before evidence of guilt was presented. These were the Sanhedrin's own rules. The members of the Sanhedrin hated Jesus so much that they rationalized that the end justifies the means and broke their own rules in their haste to condemn him to death.

The seriousness of the case was impressed upon the witnesses in cases like this: "Forget not, O witness, that it is one thing to give evidence in a trial for money and another in a trial for life. In a money suit, if thy witness-bearing shall do wrong, money may repair that wrong; but in this trial for life, if thou sinnest, the blood of the accused and the blood of his seed until the end of time shall be imputed unto thee." A chilling condemnation of those who falsely accused Jesus. They said, "Let His blood be on us and our children."

Pontius Pilate (ponchus pilot)

Pilate was the fifth procurator of the Roman province of Judaea. He held the position from 18 A. D. to 36 A. D. "A.D." is an abbreviation for Latin, "Anno Domini," which means "in the year of Our Lord." Pilate succeeded Valerius Gratus. He was deposed and sent to Rome after harshly suppressing a Samaritan uprising. He was replaced by Marcellus.

Pilate's primary functions were military, with authority over about 3,000 soldiers, and the collection of taxes. He had limited judicial functions. He was in Jerusalem during the Passover to keep order. He would do about anything to prevent an uprising.

Jesus had persuaded Levi or Matthew to quit his post as a tax collector and become one of his disciples. Jesus had exerted influence over Zacchaeus, a chief tax collector in Jericho, to resign. Earlier in the week he had run the moneychangers out of the temple. Remember that the Sanhedrin was claiming falsely that Jesus was trying to get people not to pay their taxes.

Caiaphas is looking for evidence to condemn Jesus to death but is unable to find any. The Sanhedrin wants to charge Jesus with blasphemy. However, they know that Pilate would never go for such a charge. He would simply tell them to go away and settle their own religious differences.

The conspirators settle on three charges: (1) that Jesus was a revolutionary, (2) that He incited people not to pay their taxes and (3) that He claimed to be a king. What evidence is there to support any of these charges? The answer is "none." All three charges were false. Though Jesus claimed to be a king, it was not in the sense in which he was being accused. Pilate recognized that almost immediately.

John 18:36-37 (LB) "Then Jesus answered, 'I am not an earthly king. If I were, my followers would have fought when I was arrested by the Jewish leaders. But my Kingdom is not of the world." 37. Pilate replied, 'But you are a king then?' 'Yes," Jesus said. 'I was born for that purpose. And I came to bring truth to the world. All who love the truth are my followers.'"

Luke 23:2-4 (Living New Testament) "They began at once accusing Him: 'This fellow has been leading our people to ruin by telling them not to pay their taxes to the Roman government and by claiming he is our Messiah–a King.' 3. So Pilate asked Him, 'Are you their Messiah–their King?' 'Yes,' Jesus replied. 'It is as you say.' 4. Then Pilate turned to the chief priests and to the mob and said, 'So? That isn't a crime!'"

Pilate lobbies for Jesus' to be spared. Pilate seeks to avoid responsibility for Jesus' death by washing his hands. He was reluctant to execute Jesus. His wife had warned him not to have anything to do with Jesus. He does not find anything treasonable about Jesus' actions. He repeatedly said: "I find no guilt in him."

Pilate asks Jesus if He is "King of the Jews" so he could assess Jesus' political threat. Pilate was astonished that Jesus remained silent and did not respond to the charges against Him. He tried to abdicate his responsibility by sending Jesus over to Herod.

Luke 23:8-9 (LNT) "Herod was delighted at the opportunity to see Jesus, for he had heard a lot about Him and had been hoping to see Him perform a miracle. 9. He asks Jesus question after question, but there was no reply."

Jesus admits to being a king but says, "My kingdom is not of this world

Luke 23:11 (LNT) "Now Herod and his soldiers began mocking and ridiculing Jesus; and putting a kingly robe on Him, they sent Him back to Pilate."

Pilate ultimately agrees to the execution of Jesus after the religious leaders explain that Jesus is a threat to Rome's occupation of Israel and the crowd becomes unruly. They shout, "Crucify Him!" Pilate asks, "What evil has He done?" "He's a criminal or we would not have brought him here," they reply. So much for any presumption of innocence.

John 18:29-32 (LNT) "So Pilate, the governor, went out to them and asked, 'What is your charge against this man? What are you accusing him of doing?' 30. "We wouldn't have arrested him if he weren't a criminal!' they retorted. 31. 'Then take him away and judge him yourselves by your own laws,' Pilate told them. 32.'But we want him crucified,' they said, 'and your approval is required.'"

Pilate is in a spot. The crowd is growing restless. He is afraid if he does not do what they ask, that there may be a riot. He tries to find a way out of his dilemma.

John 18:37-38 (LNT) "Pilate replied, 'But you are a king then?' "Yes,' Jesus said. 'I was born for that purpose. And I came to bring truth to the world. All who love the truth are My followers.' 38. 'What is truth?' Pilate exclaimed. Then he went out again to the people and told them, 'He is not guilty of any crime.'"

Luke 23:3-5 (LNT) "So Pilate asked Him, 'Are you their Messiah–their King?' 'Yes,' Jesus replied, 'It is as you say.' 4. Then Pilate turned to the chief priests and to the mob and said, 'So? That isn't a crime!' 5. Then they became desperate. 'But he is causing riots against the government everywhere he goes, all over Judea, from Galilee to Jerusalem!'"

Luke 23:13-16 (LNT) "Then Pilate called together the chief priests and other Jewish leaders, along with the people, 14. And announced his verdict: 'You brought this man to me, accusing him of leading a revolt against the Roman government. I have examined him thoroughly on this point and find him innocent. 15. Herod came to the same conclusion and sent him back to us–nothing this man has done calls for the death penalty. 16. I will therefore have him scourged with leaded thongs, and release him.'"

Luke 23:21-22 (LNT) But they shouted, 'Crucify him! Crucify him!' 22. Once more, for the third time, he demanded, 'Why? What crime has he committed? I have found no reason to sentence him to death. I will therefore scourage him and let him go.'"

Pilate offers to release Jesus or a known criminal, Barabbas.

John 18:39 (LNT) "But you have a custom of asking me to release someone from prison each year at Passover. So if you want me to, I'll release the 'King of the Jews.' But they screamed back, 'No! Not this man, but Barabbas.' Barabbas was a robber."

The crowd chose Barabbas. The rest is history.

Say it with me. "Crucify Him! Crucify Him!" Louder. "Crucify Him! Crucify Him!" One more time. "Crucify Him! Crucify Him!"

Can you feel it?

Can you feel the crowd as it was stirred up by the high priest and the Sanhedrin?

Do you realize that they were the same people who only five days earlier were shouting "Hosannah! Hosannah! Blessed it is the One who comes in the name of the Lord!" But they were a mob. The mob is being ruled by emotion and not by logic. A mob that somehow had been led to believe that Jesus was a fraud.

There is a fine line between love and hate. The mob crossed that line in a mere five days. "Let his blood be on us and our children!" What a horrible curse to put upon themselves and their children! And Jesus prayed, "Father, forgive them, for they know not what they are doing!"

Pilate did not have the courage to do what he knew was right and chose, instead, to go along with the crowd.

Mark 15:15 (LNT) "Then Pilate, afraid of a riot and anxious to please the people, released Barabbas to them. And he ordered Jesus flogged with a leaded whip, and handed him over to be crucified."

Luke 23:24 (LNT) "So, Pilate sentenced Jesus to die as they demanded."

Max Lucado in his book, "God Came Near," explained: "Pilate almost performed what would have been history's greatest act of mercy. He almost pardoned the Prince of Peace. He almost released the Son of God. He almost opted to acquit the Christ. Almost. He had the power. He had the choice. He wore the signet ring. The option to free God's Son was his...and he did it...almost."

What are our choices today?

When we really want something or really want an event in our lives to happen, does the end justify the means?

Do we sometimes fudge just a little?

Do we choose a form of Barabbas such as money, popularity, fame?

Or do we choose The Christ?....Almost!

Prayer

Lord, as we look at the mistakes of the past, help us to learn that the end does not justify the means. Open our hearts and minds to receive the truth that Jesus brought us. We pray in His name. Amen.

CHAPTER 2
THE SHROUD OF TURIN

In the City of Turin, Italy, today is a piece of ivory-colored linen. It is 14 feet, three inches long and three feet, seven inches wide. On the linen is the pale and subtle image of a man. It is a negative image with the dark places appearing white and the light places appearing dark. It has a history dating back more than 500 years before the invention of photography. The linen is a three-to-one herringbone twill which was used in ancient times.

The Man of Turin

The "Man of Turin," as he is sometimes called, was between 30 and 45 years of age when he died. He was 5' 11" tall and weighed 170 pounds. He was well developed with his right shoulder a little more developed than his left suggesting a manual trade of some type, perhaps a carpenter. He had long hair which was in an unbound single pigtail to the bottom of his shoulder blades. He also had a beard which suggested that he was probably a Jew because Romans were clean shaven.

On the back of his head were eight puncture wounds. There were four or five more on the front of his head suggesting that a cap of sharp objects was pressed onto his head shortly before his death. On his eyes are two coins minted by Pontius Pilate in about 30 A. D.

The Man of Turin was badly beaten before his death. Both of his eyebrows were swollen. He had a torn right eyelid. There was a large swelling below his right eye. He had a swollen nose and a triangular shaped wound on his right cheek with the apex pointing to his nose. He had a swollen left cheek and a swollen left chin.

On his back are between 90 and 120 scourge marks indicating that he was whipped shortly before his death by two men, one a little taller than the other and by one who had a tendency to whip the legs because that caused more pain. The marks are grouped in threes and perfectly match the Roman whip called a "flagellum." It is a whip with three prongs, with two of the prongs studded with metal or bone.

On his upper back, superimposed over the scourge marks, is a quadrangular shading. The crossbeam of a cross in the First Century weighed 100 pounds and could have resulted in such chafing.

Luke 23:26 (LNT) "As the crowd led Jesus away to His death, Simon of Cyrene, who was just coming into Jerusalem from the country, was forced to follow, carrying Jesus' cross."

Matthew tells us that Cyrene was in Africa.

Matthew 27:32 (LNT) "As they were on the way to the execution grounds, they came across a man from Cyrene, in Africa–Simon was his name–and forced him to carry Jesus' cross."

Four Soldiers

Jesus was led to Golgotha by four Roman soldiers.

There was a large contusion with a ragged edge to his left knee and a smaller contusion to his right knee suggesting that before his death, the Man of Turin had several falls. The road dust, travertine aragonite limestone, found on the knees and feet of the Man of Turin, is almost exclusively found in Jerusalem.

Jesus had five articles of clothing: his shoes, his turban, his girdle, his tunic, and his outer robe. Each of the soldiers got a perk for participating in a crucifixion. Each took an item of the victim's clothing. They decided not to cut the tunic into pieces but instead threw dice for it.

John 19:23 (RSV) "When the soldiers had crucified Jesus, they took his garments and made four parts, one for each soldier: also, his tunic. But the tunic was without seam, woven from top to bottom; so, they said to one another, 'Let us not tear it, but cast lots for it to see whose it shall be.' This was to fulfill the scripture, [Psalms 22:18] 'They parted my garments among them, and for my clothing they cast lots.'"

Legend has it that Mary probably had made the tunic for Jesus just before he went out into the world, before he set out on his three-year ministry. It was her last gift to her son. It was a Jewish custom to do that.

The tunic that the high priest wore was also woven from top to bottom. The Latin for "priest" was "pontifex" which means "bridge builder." The priest was supposed to be a bridge between God and his people. Jesus built that bridge as no other ever did. He was the perfect high priest.

No Broken Legs

There was no sign of broken legs, which was often done to hasten death because it would prevent the crucified man from pushing up on his feet.

John 19:32 (LNT) "So, the soldiers came and broke the legs of the two men crucified with Jesus; 33 But when they came to Him, they saw that He was dead already, so they didn't break His. 34. However, one of the soldiers pierced His side with a spear, and blood and water flowed out."

On the right side of the Man of Turin is a wound showing blood and a clear substance. The wound perfectly matches a Roman spear.

Crucifixion

The Man of Turin was crucified with his left foot crossed over his right foot and both were nailed by a single seven-inch nail.

There are wounds in both wrists. Early critics of the Shroud of Turin said that "it could not be the burial shroud of Jesus Christ," because the Bible says, "he was nailed in his hands." The Greek word for "hand" is broad enough to include the wrist.

A French doctor in the 1930's did experiments with cadavers. He hung them up nailed in the hands and found that the weight of the body caused it to pull through the nails. He nailed them in the wrists at the place shown in the Shroud of Turin and found that the nails struck the median nerve causing the thumbs to contract into the palms. In the Shroud of Turin, no thumbs are shown. It is unlikely that a forger in Medieval times would have imagined that.

Blood and Nails

The blood on the Shroud of Turin has been found to be real. It is type AB; a rare type of blood found in only 2.3% of people but as high as 18% of Jewish people. There is no image under the blood indicating that the blood was there BEFORE the image.

In 1962 an excavation of a Roman graveyard found a man who had been crucified. He still had the nails in his wrists. They were at the exact point found on the Shroud of Turin. The nails in that man had been worn on the wrists indicating that a crucified man would hang from his wrists until he could no longer bear the pain. Then he would press down on his feet to give his arms and wrists relief. When he could not stand that pain anymore, he would slump down putting the pain on his arms and wrists again. This see-sawing would happen repeatedly.

Cause of Death

The cause of death is thought to be either a heart attack caused by the blood rushing down from the upraised arms or suffocation when he could no longer push on his feet to relieve the stress on his arms and lungs of hanging by his wrists. A horrible, painful way to die.

Critics

Critics say that the Shroud of Turin cannot be real because it is so perfect in so many ways. There are more than 100 clues which support the theory that the Shroud is the burial garment of

Christ. Critics claim it had to be man-made. In Medieval times a man even confessed to having painted the image. However, modern technology has ruled out any paint pigments and any brush strokes which eliminate a painting.

One of the books I read claimed that The Shroud of Turin was actually done by Leonardo da Vinci and claimed that the image is of Leonardo himself. I have not found any actual evidence to support that theory.

Another criticism is that the Man of Turin was unwashed. It was the custom of Jews in the First Century to wash the dead. However, many victims of crucifixion were left hanging for days after their deaths for the vultures and various animals to eat the flesh. The Jewish leaders did not want the bodies of the three men who were crucified to be up during Passover.

Let's remember what happened. Christ was put on the cross at 9 a.m. Mark 15:25 (LNT) "It was about nine o'clock in the morning when the crucifixion took place."

Jesus died at 3 p.m.

Luke 23:44, 46 (LNT) "44 By now it was noon, and darkness fell across the whole land for three hours, until 3 o'clock....46 Then Jesus shouted, 'Father, I commit My spirit to You,' and with those words He died."

Joseph of Arimathaea, a member of the Sanhedrin, the Jewish Supreme Court, was the man who donated his own tomb for Christ's burial. He was late in arriving on the scene. Let's suppose he did not get there until, say, 3:30 p.m. He talks with Mary and offers his tomb. The Roman guards are not going to let anyone take the body without an order from Pontius Pilate. By now it is probably 4 p.m. Joseph, joined at some point by Nicodemus, makes the 10-minute walk from Golgotha, the place of the skull, where Jesus was crucified, to the palace of Pontius Pilate. I don't care who you are, you are going to have to wait a little while to get in to see a king. Let's suppose it is now 4:30 p.m. He has an audience with Pontius Pilate who first confirms with the centurion that Jesus is dead.

Mark 15:44 (LNT) "44 Pilate couldn't believe that Jesus was already dead so he called for the Roman officer in charge and asked him. 45 The officer confirmed the fact, and Pilate told Joseph he could have the body."

By now it is probably 4:45 p.m. or later. There will have to be an instrument drawn up and signed by Pontius Pilate. The Roman guards are not going to take anybody's word for it. That is done and signed by Pontius Pilate. Now it is sometime after 5:00 or 5:15 p.m. Joseph of Arimathaea then goes out and buys the burial shroud of Christ.

Mark 16:46 (LNT) "Joseph bought a long sheet of linen cloth and taking Jesus' body down from the cross wound it in the cloth and laid it in a rock-hewn tomb and rolled a stone in front of the entrance."

Nicodemus, gathers 100 pounds of spices.

John 19:39 (LNT) "Nicodemus, the man who had come to Jesus at night, came too, bringing a hundred pounds of embalming ointment made from myrrh and aloes."

They make their way back to Golgotha. By now it is almost 5:30 p.m. They pick up the 170 pounds of dead weight and make the normal 10-minute walk to the tomb. By now it is 5:45 p.m. or later.

They have just enough time to lay the body out, put the spices on it and wrap it in a clean linen cloth.

Matthew 27:59 (RSV) "And Joseph took the body and wrapped it in a clean linen shroud."

"John 19:40 (LNT) "Together they wrapped Jesus body in a long linen cloth saturated with the spices, as is the Jewish custom of burial."

Matthew 27:60 (LNT) "And placed it in his own new rock-hewn tomb and rolled a great stone across the entrance as he left."

Myrrh and aloe have been confirmed on the Shroud. The Sabbath would begin at 6 p.m. After 6 p.m. Friday, nobody can do any work. That is why the body was unwashed.

Carbon 14 Testing

In 1988 Carbon 14 Testing was done on the Shroud. An eight-millimeter section was cut from a corner and portions sent to three distinguished laboratories in three different countries. All three labs concluded that the Shroud dated from Medieval times, 1260 to 1390. When I first read of the Carbon 14 Testing, I was convinced that the Shroud was a forgery. It has a recorded history dated from 1365 in Lirey, France. However, I later learned that in order to have a valid test, you needed to get representative samples from the entire specimen rather than just one corner, as was done in 1988.

The reason why that is important is that in 1532 the Shroud was damaged by a fire. It was repaired by a costly process called "Invisible French Reweaving." The sample for the Carbon 14 Testing was not taken by experts but was taken by two men who were caretakers of the Shroud and who did not use gloves. One explained that he cut eight millimeters but had to discard one millimeter because it got mixed up with fibers of other origins. The other said that they discarded it because if was of a different color.

Experts examining the portion of that swatch that was taken from the Shroud have found that it contains cotton, aluminum and vanillin. None of those substances is found in the main part of the Shroud.

Vanillin

A Medieval piece of linen should retain about 37% of its vanillin. Vanillin is an extract of what produces vanilla. I mentioned to you that the sample taken from the corner has traces of vanillin in it, but the main part of the Shroud does not have any vanillin. The Dead Sea Scrolls have no vanillin in them.

The presence of vanillin, aluminum and cotton in the sample convince me that they should have taken samples from different places in the Shroud rather than just that one corner.

New Testing

In 2013 new Carbon 14 testing was done with the results that the Shroud was declared to be dated between 280 B.C. and 220 A. D. with 95% accuracy.

VP-8 Image Analyzer

Two scientists from the U. S. Air Force Academy, Dr. John Jackson and Dr. Eric Jumper, ran pictures of the Shroud through a VP-8 image analyzer. That analyzer has been used in connection with studies of the moon. If the Shroud had been a picture or a painting, it would not have three-dimensional qualifies. However, the VP-8 image analyzer showed that the Shroud has perfect three-dimensional qualities. They said that the odds that the Shroud is NOT the burial garment of Jesus are 78,000 to 1. Those are pretty good odds.

Amarillo News

In an article published by The Amarillo (Texas) News, I learned that the body of the Man of Turin showed no decomposition. The article pointed out that if the body had been unwrapped, it would have disturbed the blood stains. They would have been smeared or broken. The blood stains remained intact. To me, that suggests that Christ went through the cloth, probably in a burst of light, when he was resurrected rather than being unwrapped. To me, that explains why scientists have never been able to match or recreate the image.

Dr. Max Free

A Swiss doctor, Dr. Max Free, took a piece of tape and put it against the Shroud. Then he peeled it off and spent three years studying the fibers he found. He found that six of the fibers were consistent with fibers found only in the Holy Land.

The Shroud contains pollen from a flower that blooms only in the Jerusalem-Hebron area between March and May each year. The flower blooms only an hour a day and had to have been picked between 3 and 4 p.m.

Ultraviolet Rays

When the Shroud is put under ultraviolet rays, the parts of the Shroud burned in the 1532 fire glow. The image itself does not. Scientists are convinced that the image on the Shroud is the result of some type of scorch or light or heat, but they have not been able to reproduce the image.
A scorch would glow under radiation.

How could a corpse scorch a piece of linen? I think it was caused at the moment of Resurrection. Man cannot recreate the Resurrection. That would explain why scientists have not been able to duplicate the image.

Jeane Dixon

Jeane Dixon was a famous psychic. She said that the Shroud is real and will reveal significant truths in the 21st century. I am not a believer in psychics. I agree with a Pope who said, "People should not base their faith on a relic." I agree with Jesus who told a doubting Thomas that he believed because he had seen, but he blessed people who had not seen but still believed.

"It Is Finished!"

The first three Gospels record Jesus' last words as a "loud cry."

Matthew 27:48 (RSV) "And one of them at once ran and took a sponge, filled it with vinegar, and put it on a reed and gave it to him to drink....50 And Jesus cried again with a loud voice and yielded up his spirit."

Mark 15:36 (LNT) "So, one man ran and got a sponge and filled it with sour wine and held it up to Him on a stick....37 Then Jesus uttered another loud cry and dismissed His spirit."

Luke 23:46 (LNT) "Then Jesus shouted, "Father, I commit My spirit to You," and with those words He died."

John 19:28 (LNT) "Jesus knew that everything was now finished, and to fulfill the Scriptures said, 'I'm thirsty.' 29 A jar of sour wine was sitting there, so a sponge was soaked in it and put on a hyssop branch and held up to His lips. 30 When Jesus had tasted it, He said, 'It is finished," and bowed his head and dismissed his spirit."

That cry was not a cry of defeat. That was a loud cry of victory! His job was finished!

Also, the first two Gospels say, "vinegar put on a reed," and "sponge filled with sour wine and held up to Jesus on a stick." Luke has no mention of this. But John says they used a hyssop branch to hold the vinegar up to Jesus. What it the significance of this?

We have to go back to the original Passover, when Moses was giving the Jews instructions on how to keep their first born from being executed.

Exodus 12:1 (New International Version) "The Lord said to Moses and Aaron in Egypt ....7 Then they are to take some of the blood (of the lambs) and put it on the sides and tops of the doorframes of the houses where they eat the lambs....12 On that same night I will pass through Egypt and strike down every firstborn–both men and animals....13 The blood will be a sign for you on the houses where you are; and when I see the blood, I will pass over you. No destructive plague will touch you when I strike Egypt."

Exodus 12:21-23, 26 (NIV) "21. Then Moses...said...22 'Take a bunch of hyssop, dip it into the blood in the basin and put some of the blood on the top and on both sides of the doorframe....23 When the Lord goes through the land to strike down the Egyptians, he will see the blood on the top and sides of the doorframe and will pass over that doorway, and he will not permit the destroyer to enter your houses and strike you down....26 And when your children ask you, "What does this ceremony mean to you?' Tell them, 'It is the Passover sacrifice to the Lord, who passed over the houses of the Israelites in Egypt and spared our homes when he struck down the Egyptians."

So, the hyssop, which is a common plant of the mint family with its stiff branches and with its hairy leaves, was a good choice for sprinkling the top and sides of the door post with the "Blood of the Passover Lamb." Dr. William Barclay says, "It was the blood of the Passover Lamb which saved the people of God; it was the blood of Jesus (the Lamb of God) which was to save the world from sin."

Burial Garment Was Folded

The Bible tells us that the burial garment of Christ was folded when John and Peter went in the tomb:

John 20:6-7 (NIV) "He (Simon Peter) saw the strips of linen lying there, as well as the burial cloth that had been around Jesus' head. The cloth was folded up by itself, separate from the linen."

That has a great deal of significance. First, it is unlikely that if thieves had stolen the body that they would take the time to unwrap Jesus, much less fold Christ's burial garment and leave it in perfect order. They would be facing execution and would want to get away as quickly as possible.

Second, in the first century when a Jewish man was through with his meal, he would wad up his napkin which was a signal to his servants to come in and clear the table. However, if he was coming back, he folded his napkin.

I believe that the Shroud of Turin is real. I believe it is the burial shroud of Jesus Christ. I believe that it is solid evidence to a doubting world that Jesus Christ is who He said He is—the Son of God. I believe it is proof that he died, was buried, and rose again from the dead.

And, ladies and gentlemen, the napkin was folded... He's coming back.

Prayer:

Lord, help us to be ready when Your Son comes back. We ask in His name. Amen.

CHAPTER 3
THE MOST IMPORTANT MOMENT IN THE HISTORY OF THE WORLD

Prayer:

Good morning, Lord. Bless us now as we open ourselves to receiving Your Word.

We pray in Christ's name. Amen.

Three Gardens

There are three gardens mentioned in the Bible. Can you name them?

The Garden of Eden

Genesis 2:8 (KJV) "And the Lord God planted a garden eastward in Eden; and there he put the man whom he had formed."

What happened there? Man disobeyed God and the Devil won.

The Garden of Gethsemane

Matt. 26:36 (LNT) "Then Jesus brought them to a garden grove, Gethsemane, and told them to sit down and wait while He went on ahead to pray."

Mark 14:32 (LNT) "And now they came to an olive grove called the Garden of Gethsemane, and He instructed his disciples, 'Sit here, while I go and pray.'"

The Garden of Gethsemane. *What happened there?* Man (Jesus) obeyed God and God won.

The Third Garden?

John 20:14-16 (RSV) "Saying this she (Mary Magdalene) turned round and saw Jesus standing, but she did not know that it was Jesus. Jesus said to her, 'Woman, why are you weeping? Whom do you seek?' Supposing him to be the gardener, she said to him, 'Sir, if you have carried him away, tell me where you have laid him, and I will take him away.' Jesus said to her, 'Mary.'"

Now this is circumstantial evidence, but if Mary first thought Jesus were the gardener, why would she think that? (Because they were in a garden).

Let's look at another verse.

John 19:41 (RSV) "Now in the place where he was crucified there was a garden, and in the garden a new tomb where no one had ever been laid."

What happened in the third garden? The most historic moment in the history of the world! Mankind — that's you and I — we won. We won knowledge and absolute proof of resurrection from the dead and an assurance of eternal life.

Mary Magdalene

Let's think about Mary Magdalene at the tomb.

Why do you think Mary did not recognize Jesus?

(3) John 20:11 (RSV) "But Mary stood weeping outside the tomb..." (She was blinded by tears).

(2) John 20:14-16 (RSV) "Saying this she (Mary Magdalene) turned round and saw Jesus standing, but she did not know that it was Jesus. Jesus said to her, 'Woman, why are you weeping? Whom do you seek?' Supposing him to be the gardener, she said to him, 'Sir, if you have carried him away, tell me where you have laid him, and I will take him away.' Jesus said to her, 'Mary.'" (She was facing the wrong direction. She was facing the tomb. How many times today do we look for Jesus in the wrong direction?)

(3) She did not expect a man she knew to be dead walking around outside the tomb.

Today let's look at the resurrection through the eyes of Peter, Joseph of Arimathaea and Nicodemus.

Peter

PREPARED BIBLE STUDY LESSONS

Luke 22:61 (KJV) "Before the cock crow, thou shall deny me thrice."

So, before Christ rose, Peter denied completely even knowing Jesus. Although he walked with Jesus for three years and heard every sermon and was privy to every private insight Christ had with his disciples, he went back to fishing in a matter of days after the crucifixion. However, after the Resurrection, Peter became the leader of the disciples. When he was ultimately given the death penalty, legend has it that he said that he was not worthy to be crucified the way Christ was. So, he was crucified upside down.

The Resurrection made a dramatic difference in his life. Coming face to face with the Risen Lord will do that to you.

Arimathaea

Arimathaea was a town in Judea in 33 A.D. somewhere northwest of Jerusalem. We have no idea of its size. It no longer exists. It was probably a short distance from Jerusalem because Joseph of Arimathaea was a member of the Sanhedrin and because Joseph had purchased his tomb on the outskirts of Jerusalem.

Joseph of Arimathaea

Joseph of Arimathaea was a man of contradictions. Not much is actually known about Joseph, but he is identified as "Joseph of Arimathaea" to distinguish him from at least a dozen other "Josephs" in the Bible. He was rich. He was a Pharisee. He was a righteous man looking for the kingdom of God. He was a well-respected member of the community. He was a secret follower of Jesus because of his fear of the Jews. He was a member of the Sanhedrin, the Supreme Court of Jesus' time.

Legend says he was related to Jesus or Mary as an uncle or a great uncle. Jewish tradition was that when a person died, his nearest male relative was responsible for his burial. Thus, Jesus' father, Joseph, was present at his birth, and Joseph of Arimathaea was present at his burial.

Joseph fulfilled the prophecy in Isaiah 53:9 (NIV) "He was assigned a grave with the wicked, and with the rich in his death, though he had done no violence, nor was any deceit in his mouth."

Burial

Joseph and Nicodemus had been secret followers of Jesus up until this time. Then, they did a daring thing. They went to Pontius Pilate and begged for the body of Jesus. They both probably had fear and uncertainty. There was some risk to Joseph's reputation and for his safety. There was risk to his wealth and social status. There was risk for his life. Some Jews confronted him about what he had done and were angry with him.

Unclean

Joseph of Arimathaea would risk being "unclean" by entering the quarters of a pagan and by touching a corpse. He was probably shunned by his peers because of what he was getting ready to do.

Numbers 19:11-13 (KJV) "He that toucheth the dead body of any man shall be unclean seven days. 12 He shall purify himself with it on the third day, and on the seventh day he shall be clean, but if he purify not himself the third, then the seventh day he shall not be clean. 13 Whosoever toucheth the dead body of any man that is dead and purifieth not himself, defileth the tabernacle of the Lord; and that soul shall be cut off from Israel because the water of separation was not sprinkled upon him, he shall be unclean; his uncleanness is yet upon him."

Numbers 19:17-21 (NIV) "For the unclean person, put some ashes from the burned purification offering into a jar and pour fresh water over them. 18 Then a man who is ceremonially clean is to take some hyssop, dip it in the water and sprinkle the tent and all the furnishings and the people who were there. He must also sprinkle anyone who has touched a human bone or a grave or someone who has been killed or someone who has died a natural death. 19 The man who is clean is to sprinkle the unclean person on the third and seventh days and on the seventh day he is to purify him. The person being cleansed must wash his clothes and bathe with water, and that evening he will be clean. 20 But if a person who is unclean does not purify himself, he must be cut off from the community because he has defiled the sanctuary of the Lord. The water of cleansing has not been sprinkled on him and he is unclean. 21 This is lasting ordinance for them."

Leviticus 5:6 (KJV) "And he shall bring his trespass offering unto the Lord for his sin which he had sinned, a female from the flock, a lamb or a kid of the goats, for a sin offering; and the priest shall make an atonement for him concerning his sin."

Spices

Nicodemus bought 100 pounds of spices to bury Jesus with.

John 19:39 (LNT) "Nicodemus, the man who had come to Jesus at night, came too bringing a hundred pounds of embalming ointment made from myrrh and aloes."

Joseph of Arimathaea bought a linen shroud

Mark 15:46 (RSV) "And he bought a linen shroud, and taking him down, wrapped him in the linen shroud, and laid him in a tomb which had been hewn out of the rock."

Nicodemus and Joseph of Arimathaea went to Golgotha, "the place of the skull," to get Jesus' body and wrapped Him in the shroud with spices.

Sanhedrin

The Sanhedrin was the Jewish Supreme Court. Remember that its 70-72 sages are Scribes, Pharisees, and the Sadducees. Remember also the Sadducees maintained the temple in Jerusalem; had priestly responsibility; collected taxes; led the army; and believed in no afterlife or resurrection of the dead. The Sadducees held the majority of the seats in the Sanhedrin, but the Pharisees were popular with the people and probably controlled the voting more. The Sadducees were more concerned with politics than religion and were accommodating to Rome. Jesus called them "sons of snakes."

Let's picture some of the meetings of the Sanhedrin.

Caiaphas was the High Priest. He was also the President of the Sanhedrin. He was the person who spearheaded the conspiracy to get rid of Jesus.

Caiaphas calls the meeting of the Sanhedrin to order in the Hall of Hewn Stone, their meeting place. Somebody brings up Jesus' name. The Sadducees are particularly provoked by Jesus.

"Remember Matthew?" somebody says. "He used to be a tax collector for us. Now he is a member of that Jesus guy's gang." "What about Nicodemus?" somebody else says. "He brainwashed him into thinking he had to give back four times what he had overcharged anybody on their taxes!!" A Jewish tax collector refunding money for any reason must have been a scary thought for all of them.

One of the Pharisees probably brought up, "He refuses to keep the law. He even heals people on the Sabbath." Another probably piped up, "He even lets his band of lawbreakers break the Sabbath by picking grain on Saturdays."

Can you feel how the Sanhedrin is getting worked up?

Can you feel how uncomfortable Joseph of Arimathaea, and Nicodemus are getting?

Then somebody reminds the members of the Sanhedrin that Jesus hit them where it hurts the most–in the pocketbook.

Remember the two and a half million to three million Jews who poured into Jerusalem for the Week of the Passover brought a lot of money with them. When the people would come to the

Temple to make their Passover sacrifice, many would buy one of the 256,000 lambs that were sacrificed or a calf or a pair of doves.

Remember that these sacrifices had to be without blemish. Remember, too, that the Sadducees' Temple sacrifice inspectors would almost invariably find a blemish on any sacrifices brought by the people. Thus, they had to buy their lambs and doves from the Sadducees' representatives in the Temple.

Somebody says, "We only really get to do really big business in the Temple for seven out of the 365 days in a year. Three million people making sacrifices at a cost of say $25 each would amount to over $75 million dollars. We lost a day's sales because when Jesus overturned the tables, the money went rolling. The people stole almost every last penny. We only recovered a little bit of what fell on the floor. That rascal cost us more than $10 million dollars that day." Somebody else got really worked up. "Do you know what he said when he did that last Monday? He called our Temple a "den of thieves." Our family has been selling doves in the Temple for over 100 years. He was calling my father and my grandfather and me a thief. He was calling your families a bunch of thieves too."

John 11:48-50 (LNT) "The Chief Priests and Pharisees are saying: 'If we let him alone the whole nation will follow him—and then the Roman army will come and kill us and take over the Jewish government.' And one of them, Caiaphas, who was the High Priest that year, said, 'You stupid idiots—Let this one man die for the people—why should the whole nation perish?'"

John 18:14 (LNT) "Caiaphas was the one who told the other Jewish leaders, 'Better that one should die for all.'"

Luke 23:1 (LNT) "Then the entire Council took Jesus over to Pilate, the governor."

Note this scripture says the "entire" Council. That means all of them. 100%.

There are different theories about whether Joseph of Arimathaea was there or not. Some authorities believe that Joseph of Arimathaea did not consent to the Sanhedrin's decision and action against Jesus.

One is that "he did not take part in the resolution of the Sanhedrin to put Jesus to death." "Pictorial Bible Dictionary," The Southwestern Company, 1966, at page 449.

A second is that he was present and dissented to the Sanhedrin's decision. However, remember that the Gospel of Luke tells us that "the entire council took Jesus over to Pilate."

Luke 23:1 (LNT) "Then the entire Council took Jesus over to Pilate, the governor."

Thus, Joseph of Arimathaea and Nicodemus were probably present at Jesus' trial, but they did not speak up because of their fear of the Jews. If so, they failed to be a voice of dissent, a voice which might have given courage to others to oppose what they all knew was wrong. Their actions after the crucifixion may have been an attempt to make up for their failure to speak up.

39

Scene

Let me set the scene for you. Jesus had been building his followers. He turned water into wine. He fed 5,000 men in addition to the women and children with meager provisions. He gave Blind Bartimaeus his sight. He healed 10 lepers. He actually healed hundreds of people. He brought Lazarus back from the dead after he had been in a tomb for four days. He was rapidly gathering followers, but he was angering the establishment. He allowed his followers to pick grain and eat it on Sunday. That angered the Pharisees.

Jesus compared the Pharisees to a tomb. Pure white on the outside but full of death inside. He criticized them for not allowing people who were seeking God to find Him. Jesus healed on the Sabbath, another violation of Jewish law. But when he went into the temple and overturned the tables of the crooked moneychangers and took a whip and ran them out of the temple, the hatred of the members of the Sanhedrin for him boiled over. He hit these Jewish men, who probably received a cut of the profits, where it hurt.

Moment of Death

Matthew 27:50 (LNT) "Then Jesus shouted out again, dismissed His spirit, and died. 51 And look! The curtain secluding the Holiest Place in the Temple was split apart from top to bottom, and the earth shook, and rocks broke, 52 And tombs opened, and many godly men and women who had died came back to life again... 54 The soldiers at the crucifixion and their sergeant were terribly frightened by the earthquake and all that happened. They exclaimed, 'Surely this was God's Son.'"

Post Resurrection

According to the "Gospel of Nicodemus," Joseph of Arimathea's actions in getting Jesus' body and burying Him aroused a great deal of anger in the Jews.

"And likewise, Joseph also stepped out and said to them: Why are you angry against me because I begged the body of Jesus? Behold, I have put him in my new tomb, wrapping in clean linen; and I have rolled a stone to the door of the tomb. And you have acted not well against the just man, because you have not repented of crucifying him, but also have pierced him with a spear."

The Gospel of Nicodemus says that Joseph of Arimathaea was captured by the Jewish elders, imprisoned, and put in a cell under seal with a guard. Joseph told the other members of the Sanhedrin that Jesus would release him.

He said, "The God whom you have hanged upon the cross, is able to deliver me out of your hands." When the elders returned, the seal was still on the cell, but Joseph was gone. He had returned to Arimathaea. The elders then had a change of heart and wrote him a letter of apology and asked him what happened.

The Gospel of Nicodemus reports:

"On the day of the Preparation, about the tenth hour, you shut me in, and I remained there the whole Sabbath in full. And when midnight came, as I was standing and praying, the house where you shut me in was hung up by the four corners, and there was a flashing of light in mine eyes. And I fell to the ground trembling.

"Then someone lifted me up from the place where I had fallen, and poured over me an abundance of water from the head even to the feet, and put round my nostrils the odor of a wonderful ointment, and rubbed my face with the water itself, as if washing me, and kissed me, and said to me, Joseph, fear not; but open thine eyes, and see who it is that speaks to thee. And looking, I saw Jesus; and being terrified, I thought it was a phantom. And with prayer and the commandments I spoke to him, and he spoke with me. And I said to him: Art thou Rabbi Elias? And he said to me: I am not Elias. And I said: Who art thou, my Lord? And he said to me: I am Jesus, whose body thou didst beg from Pilate, and wrap in clean linen; and thou didst lay a napkin on my face, and didst lay me in thy new tomb, and roll a stone to the door of the tomb.

"Then I said to him that was speaking to me: Show me, Lord, where I laid thee. And he led me, and showed me the place where I laid him, and the linen which I had put on him, and the napkin which I had wrapped upon his face; and I knew that it was Jesus. And he took hold of me with his hand, and put me in the midst of my house though the gates were shut, and put me in my bed, and said to me: Peace to thee! And he kissed me, and said to me: For forty days go not out of thy house; for, lo, I go to my brethren into Galilee."

Saint Joseph of Arimathaea

The Roman Catholic Church, the Eastern Orthodox Church and some Protestant churches have venerated Joseph of Arimathaea as a saint. The traditional Roman calendar had his feast celebrated on March 17, but now do it on August 31. The Easter Orthodox Church celebrates him on the second Sunday after Easter as well as the date the Lutherans commemorate him, on July 31.

Legends

Some legends say that Joseph of Arimathaea brought Christianity to Britain and that he founded the first Christian church in Britain, but those legends have no support. Other legends associate Joseph with the Holy Grail. They claim that Joseph of Arimathaea caught some of Jesus' blood in the Cup from the Last Supper, the Holy Grail. That is also without support. It has been suggested that he was the first Bishop of Christendom.

The truth is, Joseph was probably driven to make up for any failure to speak up.

Judas

In some accounts about Joseph of Arimathaea, Judas is identified as the brother of Caiphas, who was the high priest at the time and the member of the Sanhedrin who organized the plot to kill Jesus. It was suggested that Judas infiltrated Jesus' disciples three years earlier with the intention of finding something Jesus had done that would give the Jews the ability to put him to death.

Lesson

We learned that Peter denied Christ three times yet became the "rock" on which Jesus would build his church. Joseph of Arimathaea, the man who failed to speak up at Jesus' trial, became a saint. He is the Patron Saint of Undertakers.

Thus, no matter what our sins are or how many times we fail Him, God forgives us completely each time we seek forgiveness and uses us in ways we would never dream of.

Never, never, never underestimate yourself or your ability to further the Kingdom of God.

Prayer:

Lord, help us to realize that no matter how many times we fail you, whether it be Peter, who denied Christ three times, or Joseph of Arimathaea or Nicodemus, who failed to speak up when they had the opportunity, Jesus can not only forgive us but make us a rock on which he will build His church or even a saint. He can and does use each of us regardless of our faults.

Let us strive to serve You whenever we have the chance.

We pray in Jesus' name. Amen.

CHAPTER 4
SUCCESS OR FAILURE

Prayer:

Lord, you have promised that all who seek will find. Let us then today seek You and find You. We pray in the name of the One who came to show us the way, Your Son, Jesus Christ. Amen.

Mountain Climber

There was once a young man who had as his life's ambition to climb the highest mountain. He trained for several months. He studied. He saved his money to buy the equipment and provisions for his climb.

At last, he set out on his journey. He climbed for several days. He found the climb was more difficult than he had anticipated. When he, at last, reached the timber line, he was exhausted. He was no longer able to stand up.

Across sharp rocks he continued his climb by crawling. Finally, with his last ounce of strength, he pulled himself across the top of the mountain.

And just as he did, the shadow of another mountain fell across his face, and he died.

Success or Failure

Was he a success or a failure?

The arguments for success are that he achieved his goal. He climbed the mountain.

The argument for failure is that he climbed the wrong mountain. He did not spend enough time in his preparation to determine which of two mountains, which were close together, was the highest.

Perspective

Was he a success or a failure in his own eyes?

Was he a success or a failure in the eyes of the world?

Was he a success or a failure in God's eyes?

Rodin

Auguste Rodin was a very talented French sculptor. Maybe you remember one of his most famous sculptures, "The Thinker." When he was 77 years old, France was going to dedicate a museum to his work, but, before they would do that, he had to marry Rose, the woman he had lived with for over 50 years. He did, so that he could get the museum.

Rodin and Rose had a son, who showed promise as a sculptor. However, his father never encouraged him and belittled him. He died at an early age as an alcoholic.

Was Rodin a success or a failure?

In his own eyes?

In the eyes of the world?

In God's eyes?

Can a man be a success if he is a failure to his own family?

Success or Failure

I have not been able to find the words "success" or "failure" in the Bible.

Columbus

Christopher Columbus believed that he could reach the East by sailing west. He attempted to do so but bumped into America. He never achieved his goal of reaching the East by sailing west. Yet he is credited with discovering America. His legacy has been tainted by his mistreatment of the Tiano Indians. Some he took back to Spain and sold as slaves. Others he forced to work in mines. The Taino population at the time Columbus landed was about 250,000. Yet 60 years later they became almost extinct with only a few hundred left because of mistreatment and European diseases.

Was Christopher Columbus a success or a failure?

In his own eyes?

In the eyes of the world?

In the eyes of God?

Time

Does time enter into the equation?

For example, in his own time was Christopher Columbus a success or a failure?

In modern days is Christopher Columbus considered a success or a failure?

In the eyes of God, was Christopher Columbus a success or a failure?

Adam and Eve

Genesis 3:17 (NIV) "To Adam he said, 'Because you listened to your wife and ate from the tree about which I commanded you, 'You must not eat of it,' "Cursed is the ground because of you, through painful toil you will eat of it all the days of your life.'"

Were Adam and Eve a success or failure?

Garbage Collector

A young man had as his life's ambition to become a surgeon. He had the intelligence. He had the skill. However, he got his girlfriend pregnant. He dropped out of school, married her, and became a garbage collector because that was the only job he could get at that time without an education.

Over the years he rose in the ranks to become the head of the sanitation department for the city he lived in. He instituted many changes in the ways garbage was collected and disposed of.

Was he a success or a failure?

In his own eyes?

In the eyes of the world?

In God's eyes?

The arguments for success are that he made a mistake and paid for it, but he did the best he could, worked hard at it and benefitted many people.

The arguments for failure were that he gave up his ambition, that he did not fulfill his dream, that he could have gotten scholarships to further his education, that he settled for second best.

Noah

Genesis 6:8-11 (LB) "But Noah was a pleasure to the Lord. He was the only truly righteous man living on the earth at that time. He tried always to conduct his affairs according to God's will. And he had three sons, Shem, Ham, and Japeth."

Genesis 9:20-21 (LB) "Noah became a farmer and planted a vineyard, and he made wine. One day as he was drunk and lay naked in his tent, 22 Ham, the father of Canaan, saw his father's nakedness and went outside and told his two brothers.

It appears that Noah became an alcoholic in his old age. Perhaps the visions of his friends, neighbors and family members pleading with him to let them in the ark haunted him so much that he suffered from post-traumatic stress syndrome.

Was Noah a success or a failure?

Faith

Suppose a person had as his life's ambition to climb the highest mountain of religion?

Suppose he spent his whole life studying Christianity?

He believes the scripture in John 14:6 (KJV), where Jesus says to Thomas: "I am the way, the truth and the life. No man comes to the Father but by me."

Suppose as he dies, and the mountain of Judaism or Mohammedanism falls across his face?

Is he a success or a failure?

In his own eyes?

In the eyes of the world?

In the eyes of God?

Jews

Are the Jews God's chosen people?

Deuteronomy 14:2 (RSV) "For you are a people holy to the Lord your God, and the Lord has chosen you to be a people for his own possession, out of all the peoples that are on the fact of the earth."

Did the Jews come to the Father?

Are the Jews a success or a failure?

What about the people who came before Jesus?

Twin Towers

Suppose a person had as his life's ambition to climb the mountain of Mohammedanism?

Suppose he crashes a plane into the Twin Towers in New York City and dies?

He kills over 3,000 infidels.

Is he a success or a failure?

In his own eyes?

In the eyes of the world?

In God's eye?

Jonah

Jonah 3:9-4.2 (LB) "And when God saw that they had put a stop to their evil ways, he abandoned his plan to destroy them and didn't carry it through. 4(1) This change of plans made Jonah very angry. 2 He complained to the Lord about it: 'This is exactly what I thought you'd do, Lord, when I was there in my own country and you first told me to come here."

Was Jonah a success or a failure?

In his own eyes?

In the eyes of God?

In the eyes of the world?

Optical Illusion

Would it make a difference what time of day it was when our mountain climber friend finished his climb?

For example, in the late afternoon our shadows are longer than we are. Thus, it would be possible for the shadow of a smaller mountain to fall across the face of the mountain climber making him think it were higher.

If that were true, would he be a success or a failure?

In his own eyes?

In the eyes of the world?

In God's eyes?

So, is success or failure sometime a matter of optical illusion?

Peter

Mark 14:30 (KJV) "And Jesus saith unto him, Verily I say unto thee, that this day, even in this night, before the cock crow twice, thou shalt deny me thrice."

Was Peter a success or a failure?

In his own eyes?

In the eyes of God?

In the eyes of the world?

Methodism

Let's suppose a Christian wants to climb the highest mountain of Christianity.

He studies hard and determines that Methodism is the right path to Heaven.

As he dies, the shadow of Baptism or Catholicism falls across his face.

Is he a success or a failure?

In his own eyes?

In the eyes of the world?

In God's eyes?

Ghandi

Ghandi climbed the highest mountain of Hinduism.

Was he a success or a failure?

In his own eyes?

In the eyes of the world?

In the eyes of God?

Remember Jesus said, "No man comes to the Father, except by me."

Our Responsibility

What is our responsibility?

How do we make sure we climb the highest mountain?

How do we make sure we climb the right mountain?

How do we prepare?

Answers will probably suggest that we prepare through prayer, Bible study, going to church and/or Sunday School or both, reading good literature, good works.

What is our obligation to non-believers?

Remember Jesus commanded Matthew, 28:19 (KJV): "Go ye therefore, and teach all nations."

Prayer:

Lord, as we strive to climb the highest mountain of faith, go with us on our journey. Help us to make the right decisions. We pray in the name of the One who came to show us the way. Amen.

CHAPTER 5
THOMAS

Prayer:

Lord, you know our hearts, you know our doubts, you know our good intentions. Strengthen us where we are weak as we search Your Word. We pray in Your Son's name. Amen.

Disciple

'Thomas, as you know, was one of Jesus' 12 disciples. He was probably born in Galilee.

The first reference in the Bible that I found to Thomas was in Matthew 10:2-4 and Mark 3:16-19 (LNT) "These are the names of the twelve He chose:
    Simon, (He renamed him 'Peter"),
    James and John (the sons of Zebedee, but Jesus called them,
"Sons of Thunder"),
    Andrew
    Philip
    Bartholomew,
    Matthew,
    Thomas,
    James (the son of Alphaeus),
    Thaddaeus,
    Simon (a member of a political party advocating violent
overthrow of the Roman government),
    Judas Iscariot (who later betrayed Him)."

Twin

Thomas was also called "Didymus," which is Greek meaning "the Twin." Nothing is known of his twin brother. We assume his twin was a brother. Perhaps Thomas was unsuccessful persuading his brother to follow Jesus. Sometimes we are reluctant to talk to family members about our faith. Perhaps Thomas was that way with his twin.

John 11:16 (KJV) "Then said Thomas, which is called Didymus, unto his fellow-disciples, let us also go, that we may die with him."

John 11:16 (LNT) "Thomas, nicknamed "The Twin", said to his fellow disciples, "Let's go too–and die with Him.""

So, we see that Thomas was referred to as "Didymus" or "the Twin." What Thomas is talking about is that Jesus had been hounded out of Jerusalem and sought safety in a quiet village, possibly Ephraim, which was several miles north of Jerusalem in the hills overlooking the wilderness of Judea. We don't know exactly where Jesus was at this time.

Dedication

John 10:31-33 (LNT) "31 Then again, the Jewish leaders picked up stones to kill Him. 32 Jesus said, 'At God's direction I have done many a miracle to help the people. For which one are you killing Me?" 33 They replied, 'Not for any good work, but for blasphemy; you, a mere man, have declared yourself to be God.'"

John 10:39-40 (LNT) "Once again they started to arrest Him. But He walked away and left them. 40 And went beyond the Jordan River to stay near the place where John was first Baptizing."

So, we see that Jesus was not welcome in Jerusalem and that He went some place beyond the Jordan River. But news came that Lazarus was ill.

John 11:1-3 (KJV) "Now a certain man was sick named Lazarus, of Bethany, the town of Mary and her sister Martha. 2 (Twas that Mary which anointed the Lord with ointment and wiped his feet with her hair, whose brother Lazarus was sick.) 3 Therefore his sisters sent unto him, saying, Lord, behold, he whom thou lovest is sick."

Thomas was frightened, but loyal. If Jesus were going to risk death, Thomas was going with him. The other disciples tried to persuade Jesus not to go to Bethany, which was two miles from Jerusalem, to heal Lazarus because of the danger from hostile Jews.

John 11:8 (KJV) "His disciples say unto him, Master, the Jews of late sought to stone thee; and goest thou thither again?"

John 11:8 (LNT) "But His disciples objected. 'Master,' they said, 'only a few days ago the Jewish leaders in Judea were trying to kill You. Are You going there again?'"

So, the other disciples were trying to dissuade Jesus from going back to Judea. But remember it was Thomas who said in John 11:16 (KJV), "Let us also go, that we may die with Him." If Jesus were going to risk death, Thomas was not going to try to talk Him out of it, but he was willing to die with Jesus.

Bethany

The Bible does not actually tell us that Thomas went with Jesus to Bethany, but by implication I think we can safely believe that he did.

John 11:16-17 (LNT) "'Let's go too–and die with Him.' 17 When they arrived in Bethany, they were told that Lazarus had already been in his tomb for four days."

So, I think Thomas went to Bethany. You probably remember what happened.

John 11:32 (KJV) "Jesus wept." The shortest verse in the Bible.

John 11:32 (LNT) "Tears came to Jesus' eyes."

John 11:43-44 (LNT) "Then He shouted, 'Lazarus, come out!' And Lazarus came–bound up in the burial cloth, his face muffled in a head swath. Jesus told them, 'Unwrap him and let him go!'"

So, Thomas was a witness to raising Lazarus after he had been dead for four days.

How do you think the disciples were reacting to what they saw?

Interruption

The second time Thomas is found in a significant way in the Bible is when he interrupted Jesus:

John 14:2-6 (KJV) "In my Father's house are many mansions: if it were not so, I would have told you. I go to prepare a place for you. 3 And if I go and prepare a place for you, I will come again, and receive you unto myself; that where I am, there ye may be also. 4 And whither I go ye know, and the way ye know. 5 Thomas saith unto him, Lord we know not whither thou goest; and how can we know the way? 6. Jesus saith unto him, I am the way, the truth, and the life: no man cometh unto the Father, but by me."

Thomas was a man with questions. His questions benefit all of us just the way a person's questions in a Sunday School class benefit the entire class.

John 14:4-5 (LNT) "'And you know where I am going and how to get there.' 5 'No, we don't,' Thomas said. 'We haven't any idea where You are going, so how can we know the way?'"

A great question. Jesus replied with a great answer:

John 14:6 (KJV) "Jesus saith unto him, I am the way, the truth, and the life: no man cometh unto the Father, but by me."

Thus, we have been told that our family and friends can only get to our Heavenly Father through Jesus Christ. Have we helped them understand that?

Doubting Thomas

John 20:19-20 (LNT) "That evening the disciples were meeting behind locked doors, in fear of the Jewish leaders, when suddenly Jesus was standing there among them! After greeting them, 20 He showed them His hands and side. And how wonderful was their joy as they saw their Lord!"

John 20:24-25 (LNT) "One of the disciples, Thomas, 'The Twin,' was not there at the time with the others. 25 When they kept telling him, 'We have seen the Lord,' he replied, 'I won't believe it unless I see the nail wounds in His hands–and put my fingers into them–and place my hand into His side.'"

Thomas was a "seeing is believing" type of disciple.

John 20:26-29 (LNT) "Eight days later the disciples were together again, and this time Thomas was with them. The doors were locked; but suddenly, as before, Jesus was standing among them and greeting them. 27 Then He said to Thomas, 'Put your finger into My hands. Put your hand into My side. Don't be faithless any longer Believe!' 28 'My Lord and my God!' Thomas said. 29 Then Jesus told him, 'You believe because you have seen Me. But blessed are those who haven't seen Me and believe anyway.'"

Thomas doubted so that all of us might believe.

Thomas was not with Jesus when he was crucified. Maybe he lost his nerve. Maybe in the garden of Gethsemane when Jesus told the soldiers to take him and let his disciples go, Thomas understood that they were to scatter. And scatter they did. Thomas was one of the seven disciples who went back to fishing. Jesus was only in the grave parts of three days. These disciples who had been with him for three years, these disciples who had seen Jesus heal the sick and raise the dead, these disciples who had witnessed the many miracles Jesus did, these disciples who had seen Jesus after he was resurrected were back fishing within a few days of Jesus death. Jesus had to appear to them three times before they could grasp His message.

Let's Go Fishing

John 21:1-3 (LNT) Later Jesus appeared again to the disciples beside the Lake of Galilee. This is how it happened: a group of us were there--Simon Peter, Thomas 'The Twin,' Nathanael from Cana, my brother and I and two other disciples. 3 Simon Peter said, 'I'm going fishing.'"

John 21:14 (LNT) "This was the third time Jesus had appeared to us since His return from the dead."

Commission

Matthew 28:16-20 (RSV) "Now the eleven disciples went to Galilee, to the mountain to which Jesus had directed them. 17 And when they saw him, they worshiped him; but some doubted. 18 And Jesus came and said to them, 'All authority in heaven and on earth has been given to me. 19 Go therefore and make disciples of all nations, baptizing them in the name of the Father and of the Son and of the Holy Spirit, 20 teaching them to observe all that I have commanded you; and lo, I am with you always, to the close of the age.'"

Mark 16:14-15, 20 (LNT) Still later He appeared to the eleven disciples as they were eating together. He rebuked them for their unbelief–their stubborn refusal to believe those who had seen Him alive from the dead 15 And then He told them, 'You are to go into all the world and preach the Good News to everyone, everywhere....20 And the disciples went everywhere preaching, and the Lord was with them and confirmed what they said by the miracles that followed their messages."

Additional Thoughts on Thomas

John 20:28 (LNT) "My Lord and my God." All of Thomas' fears and doubts are swept away.

"Thomas's lack of faith did more for our faith than did the faith of the disciples who believed," Pope Gregory, the Great, in the Sixth Century, A. D.

He went fishing in the Sea of Galilee with six other disciples after Jesus' death and was there when Jesus appeared. John 21:1-8.

He was in the Upper Room in Jerusalem after the Ascension when the disciples elected a replacement, Matthias, for Judas. Acts 1:13, 25.

According to tradition, Jesus' words were recorded by only four of His disciples: Matthew, John, Phillip and Thomas. The Gospel of Thomas was probably written by him. It is not included in the Christian Bible. It was found in 1945 in Nag Hammadi in upper Egypt in a cache of hidden manuscripts.

Excerpts from the Gospel of Thomas:

Jesus said, "Whoever is near me is near the fire, and whoever is far from me is far from the kingdom."

They said unto Him, "Come and let us pray today and let us fast." Jesus replied, "Which then is the sin I have committed, or in what have I been vanquished?" Or, later, "Which of you convicts me of sin?"

"Life is a bridge. You pass over it but build no houses on it."

"Blessed is the man who suffers. He finds life." A new Beatitude.

Jesus reproached the Pharisees by saying: "Woe to them, for they are like a dog sleeping in a manger of oxen, for neither does he eat nor allow the oxen to eat."

"See the sower went out, he filled his hand, he threw. Some seed fell on the road, the birds came, they gathered them. Others fell on the rock, and did not strike root in the earth, and did not produce ears. Others fell in the thorns. They choked the seed, and the worm ate them. Others fell on the good earth and brought forth good fruit. It bore sixty per measure and one hundred and twenty per measure."

According to tradition, after Jesus died, Thomas went to Parthia, Persia and India. Mount Thomas in India is named after this disciple.

Prayer:

Lord, forgive us when we doubt, just as You forgave Doubting Thomas. As we seek you, Lord, strengthen us for the journey. Amen.

CHAPTER 6
AM I MY BROTHER'S KEEPER?

Prayer:

Lord, today as we explore our responsibility to others, open our hearts, minds, and ears to your Word. We pray in Jesus' name. Amen.

My Friend John

I grew up in the 1300 block of Christine Street in Pampa, Texas, a half block from the high school. When I was in high school, it fell my lot to pump up all the footballs and basketballs in the neighborhood. That wasn't because I was such a good guy. I had the only pump on the block.

John was in grade school and lived about three houses down from me. His father was our Postmaster. He had an older brother, Jackie, who was two years older than I, and he had a sister, Wynell, who was my age. One day he brought me his basketball to pump up. I pumped it up and handed it back to him. He tossed it up and down on his hand. He got this look on his face, like, he was going to ask me a question. Sure enough, he did.

"Scooter," he said. That was my nickname. "Yeah, John," I responded. "Why did you spit on the needle?" he asked.

"To moisten it a little," I explained. "That makes the needle go into the ball a little easier and helps keep it from bending."

"Oh," he said and got this funny look on his face. "I always did it because you did it, but I always wondered why."

As he walked away, I was a little shaken. I thought to myself, "If he is watching my life so closely that he would spit on a needle because I did, what else would he do, simply because I did it?"

Psychologists

Psychologists tell us that all of us have someone like John in our lives. All of us have someone who looks up to us and tries to be like us. They will follow our example. It may be a son or daughter. It may be a grandson or granddaughter. It may be someone at work. It may be that kid down the street who is a nuisance.

Think with me a moment. Who is that person "John" in your life?

Climbers

A father and his son were climbing a mountain. When they got to a steep part, the footing was uncertain. So, the father made sure his son was putting his feet everywhere the father did. "Be careful, Dad," the boy told him. "Remember, I'm following in your footsteps." The son was looking up to his father the way John was looking up to me.

Genesis 4:9 (KJV) "And the Lord said unto Cain, Where is Abel thy brother? And he said, I know not: Am I my brother's keeper?"

Genesis 4:9 (LB) "But afterwards the Lord asked Cain, 'Where is your brother? Where is Abel?' 'How should I know?' Cain retorted. 'Am I supposed to keep track of him wherever he goes?'"

These are examples of how many people have someone else who looks up to them.

Brother's Keeper

How should we respond to that question today: Am I my brother's keeper?

Who Is My Brother?

Who is my brother?

An obvious answer is a family member.

What are some examples of brothers in the Bible?

63

Jacob and Esau: Genesis 25:29-34 (KJV) "And Jacob sod pottage: and Esau came from the field, and he was faint: 30 And Esau said to Jacob, Feed me, I pray thee, with that same red pottage; for I am faint: therefore was his name called Edom. 31 And Jacob said, Sell me this day thy birthright. 32 And Esau said, Behold, I am at the point to die: and what profit shall this birthright do to me? 33 And Jacob said, "Swear to me this day; and he swore unto him: and he sold his birthright unto Jacob. 34 Then Jacob gave Esau bread and pottage of lentils; and he did eat and drink, and rose up, and went his way: Thus, Esau despised his birthright."

Joseph's brothers sold him into slavery, Genesis 37:26-29 (KJV): "And Judah said unto his brethren, What profit is it if we slay our brother, and conceal his blood? 27 Come, and let us sell him to the Ishmeelites, and let not our hand be upon him; for he is our brother and our flesh. And his brethren were content. 28 Then there passed by Midianites merchantmen; and they drew and lifted up Joseph out of the pit, and sold Joseph to the Ishmeelites for twenty pieces of silver: and they brought Joseph into Egypt."

James and John were the sons of Zebedee, Luke 5:10-11 (KJV): "And so was James, and John, the sons of Zebedee, which were partners with Simon. And Jesus said unto Simon, Fear not; from henceforth thou shalt catch men. 11 And when they had brought their ships to land, they forsook all, and followed him."

Andrew brought his brother, Peter, to Christ, John 1:40-42 (KJV): "One of the two which heard John speak, and followed him, was Andrew, Simon Peter's brother. 41 He first findeth his own brother Simon, and saith unto him, We have found the Messiah, which is, being interpreted, the Christ. 42 And he brought him to Jesus. And when Jesus beheld him, he said, Thou art Simon the son of Jonah: thou shalt be called Cephas, which is by interpretation, A stone."

Thomas, we learned last week, was also called Didymus, which is Greek for Twin. He apparently was not able to persuade his twin to follow Christ.

John 11:16 (KJV) "Then said Thomas, which is called Didymus, unto his fellow-disciples, Let us also go, that we may die with him."

John 11:16 (LNT) "Thomas, nicknamed "The Twin", said to his fellow disciples, "Let's go too–and die with Him."

Who else is my brother?

Deuteronomy 23:6-7 (LB) "You must never, as long as you live, try to help the Ammonites or the Moabites in any way. 7 But don't look down on the Edomites and the Egyptians; the Edomites are your brothers and you lived among the Egyptians."

So, neighbors can be considered brothers. The Edomites were descendants of Esau and were neighbors to the Jews.

What About All Mankind?

Matthew 18:35 (RSV) "So also my heavenly Father will do to every one of you, if you do not forgive your brother from your heart."

1 John 3:15-16 (LNT) "Anyone who hates his Christian brother is really a murderer at heart; and you know that no one wanting to murder has eternal life within. 16 We know what real love is from Christ's example in dying for us. And so, we also ought to lay down our lives for our Christian brothers."

Mark 3:31-35 (NIV) "Then Jesus' mother and brothers arrived. Standing outside, they sent someone in to call him. 32 A crowd was sitting around him, and they told him, 'Your mother and brothers are outside looking for you.' 33 'Who are my mother and my brothers?' he asked. 34 Then he looked at those seated in a circle around him and said, 'Here are my mother and my brothers! 35 Whoever does God's will is my brother and sister and mother.'"

So, would my neighbor John be my brother?

Are all men my brothers?

Duty

I was privileged to teach Sunday School in our church for 50 years. I spent about 25 years in the Senior High Department and about 25 years in the Junior High Department. In the Senior High Department, a young lady abruptly quit coming to Sunday School. I probably called her several times and may have even written to her, but I never got an answer or even a response as to why.

About three years later, her grandmother came to see me on some legal business. She brought up the subject. "John, do you know why my granddaughter quit coming to your Sunday School Class?"

"No," I responded. "I've wondered why." "She thinks you are a hypocrite," the lady told me. "She said that you told your Sunday School Class that you did not drink or smoke. Yet she saw you drinking beer at a Jaycee party. After that, she never came back!"

"I don't drink or smoke," I assured her. "I never have! I don't understand."

I really struggled to remember what she was talking about. I finally remembered. My wife and I love to dance. We were members of the Pampa Jaycees when we first moved back to Pampa after I finished law school. We went to a Jaycee party to dance. My class member was part of the band. I remembered that Judy and I both drank cokes out of a Budweiser cup that evening.

She must have seen me drinking from the Budweiser cup and thought I was drinking beer when I actually was only drinking a coke!

What duty to I owe to my brother?

When I think of what I should do, I think of First Thessalonians 5:22.

1 Thessalonians 5:22 (KJV) "Abstain from all appearance of evil."

How do we do that?

Churchill

During World War II, just when things were the darkest for England. Just when Hitler was threatening to cross the English Channel. Just when England was enduring nightly bombing raids. Just at that most inopportune time, the miners announced to Prime Minister Winston Churchill that they were going on strike.

Churchill, called the President of the Union and tried to get him to allow him to speak to the miners. "It's no use," the man told him. "We're unnoticed, unappreciated and underpaid." But he agreed for Churchill to speak.

That night Churchill entered the union hall. There was a single aisle separating the angry miners as Churchill made his way to the front of the hall.

He went to the podium, turned around and looked out at the miners. Gentlemen," he began in that magnificent voice of his. "There will come a day, tomorrow perhaps, when our time will be over, and the battle will be done. And on that day, each of us will be required to march past a reviewing stand. And on that reviewing stand will be the people of England.

"And the soldier will be required to stop, individually, and face the reviewing stand and answer this question, 'Where were you when your country needed you?' And the soldier will answer: 'Where was I when my country needed me? I was in the trenches.'

"And the sailor will answer: 'Where was I when my country needed me? I was on the ships.'"

"And the miner - ah, the miner - will answer: "Where was I when my country needed me? I was in the pits. Unnoticed, unappreciated, and underpaid. But when my county needed me, I was where I could serve her best.'"

Ladies and gentlemen, I believe there will come a day - tomorrow perhaps - when our time will be over and the battle will be done. And on that day, each of us will be required to march past a reviewing stand. And on that reviewing stand will be our Lord and Savior, Jesus Christ, and His Father, God. And each of us will be required to stop, individually and face the reviewing stand and answer this question. "Where were you when God needed you?"

And the missionary will answer, "Where was I when God needed me? I was in the mission field bringing the Word of God to people who otherwise would not have heard it."

And the minister will answer, "Where was I when God needed me? I was visiting the sick and dying and praying with them."

And now it's your turn. You stop. Individually. You face the reviewing stand. Comes the question: "Where were you when God needed you?"

What will be your answer?

Prayer:

Pray with me, please. Lord, help us to be Christian examples to others and to be where You need us to be when You need us to be. We pray in the name of Your Son, who, indeed, was where You wanted Him to be, when You wanted Him to be. Amen.

CHAPTER 7
PACERS

Prayer:

Lord, this morning we ask you to show us the way You want us to go. We pray in Jesus' name. Amen

Chris Chataway

Have you ever heard of Chris Chataway? Does it ring any bells?

Now what if I were to say, "Have you ever heard of Roger Bannister?" If you were a track fan, you might say, "Sure. Roger Bannister was an English medical student who was the first person to break a four-minute mile. He did it on May 6, 1954. His time was 3.59.4 seconds. You might even remember that there was a movie about his life a few years ago called "The Four Minute Mile."

John Landy

What if I were to ask about John Landy? Some of you might say, "He was a butterfly chaser from Australia and was the second person to break the four-minute mile." He did it on June 21, 1954, with a time of 3.58 seconds flat.

Mile of the Century

They ran against each other on August 7, 1954, in what was termed "The Mile of the Century." The world was amazed. Both men ran the mile at less than four minutes with Bannister winning with a time of 3.58.8 seconds.

Pacer

But Chris Chataway? Chris Chataway was a pacer. The pacer runs on the lane outside of the star. He actually runs more than a mile because the star has the inside track which is exactly a mile. The pacer's job is to set the right pace so the star can do his best.

Roger Bannister had a unique kick at the end of a race. He believed if he could run three-fourths of a mile in three minutes, that he could use his famous kick to beat the clock in the last quarter of a mile. Chris Chataway trained by his side for three years learning to run three quarters of a mile in three minutes. And on May 6, 1954, Roger Bannister's time at the three-quarter mark was exactly three minutes.

Six weeks later he was flown to the side of John Landy and paced him to a new world record in the mile. Still later he paced another man to a record in the two-mile run and finished so closely behind him that he was given the same time.

The world heard again from Chris Chataway when three men broke the four-minute mile in the same race. And the number three man....was the pacer, Chris Chataway.

Chris Chataway was a person who had the ability to run a four-minute mile, yet he was able to put his own ambitions in the background to pace other runners to even greater accomplishments.

Would you agree with me if I were to say, "We need more pacers in our church?"

Peter

When Jesus' disciples are mentioned, many people think of Peter first. Yet if it were not for his brother, Andrew, the world might never have heard of Peter.

What did Andrew do?

Andrew brought his brother, Peter, to Christ, John 1:40-42: (KJV) "One of the two which heard John speak, and followed him, was Andrew, Simon Peter's brother. 41 He first findeth his own brother Simon, and saith unto him, We have found the Messiah, which is, being interpreted, the Christ. 42 And he brought him to Jesus. And when Jesus beheld him, he said, Thou art Simon the son of Jonah: thou shalt be called Cephas, which is by interpretation, A stone."

Thomas, we learned last week, was also called Didymus, which is Greek for Twin. He apparently was not able to persuade his twin to follow Christ. Note that Andrew was the first disciple to realize that Jesus was the Messiah. "We have found the Messiah."

Andrew

There are only 12 references to Andrew in the Bible. One-third of them are simply a list of the disciples. When he is mentioned, his brother, Peter, is always mentioned first. Further, Peter is never referred to as "Andrew's brother." It is always, Andrew being referred to as "Simon Peter's brother."

Is this significant? It would seem to indicate that he was younger or less important. Yet he is referred to as "Saint Andrew."

The name, "Andrew," means "manly" or "courage."

We know almost nothing about his father, Jonah.

We know that Andrew was a fisherman.

Matthew 4:18 (KJV) "And Jesus, walking by the sea of Galilee, saw two brethren. Simon called Peter, and Andrew his brother, casting a net into the sea: for they were fishers."

Matthew 4:18 (LNT) "One day as He was walking along the beach beside the Lake of Galilee, He saw two brothers–Simon, also called Peter, and Andrew– (on a boat) fishing with a net, for they were commercial fisherman."

Andrew was from Bethsaida (Beth-say-duh).

John 1:44 (LNT) (Phillip was from Bethsaida, Andrew, and Peter's hometown.)

Andrew was first a disciple of John the Baptist and was the first disciple of Jesus.

John 1:35-40 (LNT) "The following day as John was standing with two of his disciples, 36 Jesus walked by. John looked at Him intently and then declared, 'See! There is the Lamb of God!' 37 Then John's two disciples turned and followed Jesus! 38. Jesus looked around and saw them following. 'What do you want?' He asked them, 'Sir,' they replied, 'where do You live?' 39 'Come and see,' He said. So, they went with Him to the place where He was staying and were with Him from about four o'clock that afternoon until the evening. 40 (One of these men was Andrew, Simon Peter's brother.)"

The Bible tells us that Andrew was one of the disciples who had questions about the Temple.

Mark 13:1-4 (LNT) "As He was leaving the Temple that day, one of His disciples said, 'Teacher, what beautiful buildings these are! Look at the decorated stonework on the walls.' 2

Jesus replied, 'Yes, look! For not one stone will be left upon another, except as ruins.' 3-4 And as He sat on the slopes of the Mount of Olives across the valley from Jerusalem, Peter, James, John, and Andrew got alone with Him and asked him, 'Just when is all this going to happen to the Temple? Will there be some warning ahead of time?'"

Andrew was a pacer. He was a facilitator. As we said, he brought his brother, Simon Peter, to Jesus. He also brought other people.

John 12:20-22 (LNT) "Some Greeks who had come to Jerusalem to attend the Passover 21 Paid a visit to Phillip, who was from Bethsaida, and said, 'Sir, we want to meet Jesus.' 22 Philip told Andrew about it, and they went together to ask Jesus."

Andrew does not do great things himself, but he sets them in motion–like a pacer or facilitator should do. Remember when Jesus fed 5,000 men, not including the women and children?

John 6:5-9 (RSV) "Lifting up his eyes, then; and seeing that a multitude was coming to him, Jesus said to Philip, 'How are we to buy bread, so that these people may eat?' 6 This he said to test him, for he himself knew what he would do Philip answered him, 'Two hundred denarii would not buy enough bread for each of them to get a little.' 8 One of his disciples, Andrew, Simon Peter's brother, said to him, 'There is a lad here who has five barley loaves and two fish; but what are they among so many?'"

You will remember that Jesus had the multitude sit down. He divided the five barley loaves and two fish among the people and had 12 baskets full left over, one for each disciple.

The last reference in the Bible to Andrew comes in Acts 1. He is present and voting on Matthias to replace Judas as one of the disciples.

After Jesus' resurrection, Simon Peter and six other disciples went fishing. Jesus appeared to them.

John 21:2-3 (LNT) "A group of us were there–Simon Peter, Thomas 'The Twin,' Nathaniel from Cana, in Galilee, my brother James and I and two other disciples. 3 Simon Peter said, 'I'm going fishing.' 'We'll come too,' we all said. We did but caught nothing all night."

Jesus had them throw their nets in again and they caught so many fish that they could not even bring them all in. They caught 153 large fish without tearing the net.

Did you notice something?

John only named five of the seven disciples. If Andrew were one of the other two, John must not have considered him very important because he did not even mention him by name!

After Jesus' resurrection, many centuries of church tradition says that Andrew was sent to Scythia (an ancient region in central Eurasia). A much later work added that he preached in regions surrounding the Black Sea. And an ancient apocryphal text claimed he preached in Achaea, sometimes spelled Achaia (a region in Greece).

Andrew was one of the earliest evangelists.

Tradition says that Andrew was crucified in about 60 A.D. on an X shaped cross and was bound, not nailed, to it. According to the "Acts of Andrew," he preached from the cross for three days before he died.

Andrew's death inspired what is known as "the St. Andrew's cross," an X shaped cross.

Grocery Store

My daughter was in a grocery store a few days ago. A lady had a toddler in her basket. As they passed things in the store and she would put them in her basket, the lady would say, "apple," "banana," "lettuce," "tomato." She had her daughter repeat what she pointed out each time.

This lady was pacing her child's learning by starting early.

Time

Andrew was Jesus' first disciple. He was also one of the world's first evangelists.

His life brings up the question: "When is the time to serve?" Let's think together.

Mary gave birth to Jesus when she was 14. George Westinghouse invented the rotary engine when he was 15. John C. Hall and his brothers created Hallmark Cards when they were teenagers. Johnny Campbell, when he was a senior at Pampa High School, managed the campaign for re-election of a United States Congressman.

George Washington fought his first battle as a Lieutenant Colonel at the age of 22. William Pitt the Younger was Prime Minister of England at 24. Charles Lindberg flew the Spirit of St. Louis and became a national hero when he was the first man to fly across the Atlantic Ocean. He was 25.

Jesus Christ began his short three-year ministry at the age of 30. Martin Luther nailed his famous thesis to the door when he was 34. By the time Julius Caesar was 35, he had conquered 800 cities, 300 nations and three million men.

John Glenn was 40 when he became the first American to circle the earth in space. John F. Kennedy became President of the United States when he was 43. Abraham Lincoln had a history of failures until he won the Presidency when he was 51.

Jay Morgan made his first million at the age of 60. If Winston Churchill had died when he was 64, nobody would have ever remembered him. He became Prime Minister of England at the age of 65.

Bob Dole sought the Presidency in his 70s. Ronald Regan was past 80 when he completed his second term. I read about a woman who wrote a best seller when she was 88. It was the first book she had ever written.

I saw Bob Hope give national television specials when he was in his 90s. George Burns had a contract to play Las Vegas on his 100th birthday.

The New English Version of the Bible in Psalms 92:14 says: "The righteous will still bear fruit in old age."

Tom Brady is famous for his fourth quarter comebacks. Many of us are in the fourth quarter of life. When is the time to serve?

The time to serve is now. Last week we were asked, "Where were you when God needed you?" Now is the time to compose your answer by doing.

James 2:17 (LNT) "So, you see, it isn't enough just to have faith. You must also do good to prove that you have it. Faith that doesn't show itself by good works is no faith at all–it is dead and useless."

James 2:17 (KJV) "Even so faith, if it hath not works, is dead, being alone."

Philippians 2:3-4 (NIV) "In humility value others above yourselves, not looking to your own interests but each of you to the interests of the others."

Abilities, Inc.

In New York City is a corporation called, "Abilities, Inc." It only hires people who are disabled. If you were to visit the CEO, he would come out from behind his desk in a wheelchair to greet you. If you were to make the mistake of calling the company, "Disabilities, Inc.," he would correct you in a hurry.

"Can you take a car, disassemble it and put it back together, blindfolded? "If you say, "No," he will respond, "You are kind of handicapped, aren't you?" We have people who work here who do that every day. "We concentrate on our abilities, not our disabilities."

So, all of us need to do that. We need to concentrate on what we can do for Christ. Not what we cannot do.

My friend, Ramona, has multiple sclerosis. When she lived in Pampa, I remember that I got a call from her on my birthday. She said, "John, on behalf of the First United Methodist Church, I want to wish you a happy birthday." She did that for every single member of our church during all the years that she and her family lived in Pampa. She could use the telephone to serve Christ. She concentrated on what she could do rather than lament what she could not do.

Melba is an inspiration to me. Though she is partially blind, she rarely misses church. She sings in the choir. The rest of us have the music in front of us. Melba has to memorize the music each week because she cannot see well enough to read the music.

Melba is a "can do" person. She concentrates on what she can do rather than what she cannot do.

Prayer:

Lord, help us to be inspired by the example of Andrew. Let us be the pacers who lead others to Christ. We pray in Your Son's Name. Amen.

CHAPTER 8
WAS JESUS SERIOUS?

Prayer:

Lord, help us listen for Your Word today and help us to act on it. In the name of the One who came to show us the way. Amen.

Texas A&M

When I was a freshman at Texas A&M University and was standing in formation a few days into the first semester, our First Sergeant bellowed, "Freshmen! Look at the man on your left." We did. Then he said, "Look at the man on your right." We did again. Then he emphasized, "Neither one of them will be there when you graduate!" We reacted. Then he said, "But remember, two guys were looking at you1"

My roommate, a guy from Dallas, tried hard, but he did not make it. He was an aeronautical engineering major. He flunked out of school. He transferred to Baylor University, graduated, and ultimately became a commercial airline pilot for Braniff International Airways.

Even though he really wanted to graduate from Texas A&M and had a strong desire, he did not make the grade and was passed over. My Sergeant wound up being right. Only a third of our freshman class actually graduated.

Boys Scouts

When I was a Boy Scout, I was chosen for the "Order of the Arrow." We were told, "Many are called, but few are chosen."

Matthew 22:14 (KJV) "For many are called, but few are chosen."

Why do you think that is?

Is that true in other areas of our lives?

Businesses

Think of some businesses both nationally and locally which are no longer in our community.

What did they all have in common?

(Some lasted a short time. Others were in business a long time. However, they have all closed.)

Does every business that tries hard make it?

Does every Christian who tries hard make it?

John 14

John 14.6 (KJV) "Jesus said unto him (Thomas), 'I am the way, the truth, and the life: no man cometh unto the Father, but by me.'"

John 14:6 (LB) "Jesus told him (Thomas), 'I am the Way–yes, and the Truth and the Life. No one can get to the Father except by means of me.'"

John 14:6 (NIV) "Jesus answered, 'I am the way and the truth and the life. No one comes to the Father except through me.'"

Was Jesus serious? Is there only one narrow path, one door, one way to Heaven?

Matthew 7

Matthew 7:13-14 (KJV) "Enter ye in at the strait gate: for wide is the gate, and broad is the way, that leadeth to destruction, and many there be which go in thereat. Because strait is the gate, and narrow is the way, which leadeth unto life, and few there be that find it."

Matthew 7:13-14 (LB) "Heaven can be entered only through the narrow gate! The highway to hell is broad, and its gate is wide enough for all the multitudes who choose its easy way. But the gateway to Life is small, and the road is narrow, and only a few ever find it."

What does this mean?

I read not long ago, that about 107 billion people have lived on earth at one time or another. Now if only a few of those people find their way, then more than half will enter eternity through the broad gate.

But think with me now.

Funerals

Have you ever been to a funeral where the preacher suggested that the deceased was not in Heaven with Jesus?

I went to the funeral of an atheist once. He had hung himself after a life that included using and selling drugs. There was no suggestion that he was not going to Heaven.

I also attended the funeral of a man who got messed up on drugs. He went from Texas to another state to do bodily harm to the man who married his divorced wife. He wound up getting shot and killed in a standoff with law enforcement officers.

The preacher at his funeral said, "I hope that you will forgive him. God already has."

Do you agree with these ministers?

When God judges our lives, what criteria will He use?

Does He judge our entire life or just the last few minutes?

What about the thief on the cross?

Luke 23:39-43 (LB) "One of the criminals hanging beside him scoffed, 'So you're the Messiah, are you? Prove it by saving yourself–and us, too, while you're at it!' 40 But the other thief protested. 'Don't you even fear God when you are dying? We deserve to die for our evil deeds, but this man hasn't done one thing wrong.' Then he said, 'Jesus, remember me when you come into your Kingdom.' 43 And Jesus replied, 'Today you will be with me in Paradise. This is a solemn promise.'"

A solemn promise. I'll wager that the thief was glad God did not measure him by his entire life. Something you might make note of: This is the only time in the Bible that someone calls Jesus by his first name. Only a thief on the cross did it.

Do you remember the parable of the workers?

Matthew 20:1-16 (LB) "Here is another illustration of the Kingdom of Heaven. 'The owner of an estate went out early one morning to hire workers for his harvest field. 2 He agreed to pay them $20 a day and sent them out to work. 3 A couple of hours later he was passing a hiring hall and saw some men standing around waiting for jobs, 4 so he sent them also into his fields, telling them he would pay them whatever was right at the end of the day. 5 At noon and again around three o'clock in the afternoon he did the same thing. 6 At five o'clock that evening he was in town again and saw some more men standing around and asked them, 'Why haven't you been working today?'

7 'Because no one hired us,' they replied. 'Then go on out and join the others in my fields,' he told them. 8 That evening he told the paymaster to call the men in and pay them, beginning with the last men first. 9 When the men hired at five o'clock were paid, each received $20. 10 So when the men hired earlier came to get theirs, they assumed they would receive much more. But they, too, were paid $20.

11-12 They protested. 'Those fellows worked only one hour, and yet you've paid them just as much as those of us who worked all day in the scorching heat." 13 'Friend,' he answered one of them. 'I did you no wrong! Didn't you agree to work all day for $20? 14 Take it and go. It is my desire to pay all the same; 15 Is it against the law to give away my money if I want to? Should you be angry because I am kind?' 16 And so it is that the last shall be first, and the first last."

What is the meaning of this parable?

God's Memory

If God is perfect, does that mean God has a good memory, a perfect memory?

Think about your own children a moment.

Can you think of anything they might do which would cause you to condemn them to Hell?

If God is a perfect and forgiving father, do you think He would do less?

There are several passages in the Bible that indicate that God forgives and forgets our sin.

Psalm 103:12 (KJV) "As far as the east is from the west, so far hath he removed our transgressions from us."

Psalm 103:12 (LB) "He has removed our sins as far away from us as the east is from the west."

Isaiah 43:25 (NIV) "I, even I, am he who blots out your transgressions, for my own sake, and remembers your sins no more."

Hebrews 10 explains that Jesus' death on the cross was for all of us. It was a once-and-for-all type of sacrifice for our sins. He made a complete payment. We don't have to continue to sacrifice like they did in the Old Testament.

Hebrews 10:14–18 (NIV) "Because by one sacrifice he has made perfect forever those who are being made holy. The Holy Spirit also testifies to us about this. First, he says: 'This is the covenant I will make with them after that time, says the Lord. I will put my laws in their hearts, and I will write them on their minds.' Then he adds: 'Their sins and lawless acts I will remember no more.' And where these have been forgiven, sacrifice for sin is no longer necessary."

If God forgives and/or forgets our sins, does that mean everybody gets in?

If God forgives our sins, what criteria does He use to judge us on Judgment Day?

Children

Matthew 18:2 (LB) "Jesus called a small child over to him and set the little fellow down among them, and said, 'Unless you turn to God from your sins and become as little children, you will never get into the Kingdom of Heaven.'"

What did he mean by that?

Remember what Paul said to us in 1 Corinthians 13:11 (LB): "It's like this - when I was a child I spoke and thought and reasoned as a child does. But when I became a man, my thoughts grew far beyond those of my childhood, and now I have put away the childish things."

Are these thoughts consistent?

A Christmas Story

Last week I came across a story by Terry Hudson of Houston.

It was five days before Christmas. Cars packed the parking lot of a Houston area Target Shopping Center. It had not been a good day. His feet ached. His head hurt. He made several purchases and then got in what he thought was the shortest line–it was a 20-minute wait.

In front of him were two small children. The boy was about 10. The girl was about 5. The boy had on a ragged coat and enormously large, tattered tennis shoes. The shoes jutted far out in front of his much too short jeans. He clutched several crumpled dollars in his grimy hands. The girl's clothing resembled her brother's. Her head was a matted mess of curly hair. Part of her evening meal showed on her small face. She was carrying a beautiful pair of shiny, gold house slippers. She was humming happily, though a little off key, to the music playing over the store's loud speakers.

When they finally got to the checkout stand, the girl carefully placed the shoes on the counter. She treated them as though they were a treasure. The clerk rang up the bill. "That will be $6.09, please," she said. The boy laid his crumpled dollars in front of the clerk while he searched his pockets. He came up with $3.12.

"I guess we'll have to put them back," he bravely told his sister. She broke into a soft sob. "But Jesus would have loved these shoes," she cried. "Well, we'll go home and work some more. Don't cry. We'll come back," he promised.

Mr. Hudson quickly handed $3 to the cashier. He was thinking that these children had waited in line a long time. After all, it was Christmas. Suddenly a pair of arms came around him and a small voice said, "Thank you, Sir."

"What did you mean when you said Jesus would love these shoes?" he asked. The small boy answered, "Our Mommy is sick and going to Heaven. Daddy said she might go before Christmas to be with Jesus." The little girl spoke up, "My Sunday School teacher said that the streets in Heaven are shiny gold, just like these slippers. Won't Mommy be beautiful walking on those streets to match these shoes?"

"Yes," he answered. His eyes flooded as he looked into the tear-streaked face. "I am sure she will."

The faith of a child. That is the kind of faith Jesus was talking about. Terry Hudson learned from two children about having love in your heart. About sharing. About giving.

Grace

I once read an article about a lawyer who worked his way through law school by being a waiter at Red Lobster. He said one night he gave perfect service to a table. Their water glasses were never less than half full when he refilled them. He got their salads to them immediately and their main meal a short time later. They left him a $20 tip. He felt he earned it.

That same night, he actually forgot about another table. He was late in bringing their menus. He was late in turning in their orders. He knew he was not going to get a tip, so he concentrated on his other tables. He felt badly that he had given them poor service. They left him a $20 tip.

He felt that he did not earn it. But it helped him understand grace. We may not deserve God's grace. We cannot be good enough to earn it. We may not understand it. But Grace is available to all of us if we confess our sins and ask for forgiveness and God's Grace.

Romans 4:16 (LB) "So, god's blessings are given to us by faith, as a free gift; we are certain to get them whether or not we follow Jewish customs if we have faith like Abraham's, for Abraham is the father of us all when it comes to these matters of faith."

Romans 3:23-24 (KJV) "For all have sinned, and come short of the glory of God; 24 Being justified freely by his grace through the redemption that is in Christ Jesus."

It's not a matter of money. It's not the number of good deeds we do. It is a relationship that we only have to accept to receive.

Prayer:

Lord, come into our hearts. Come into our lives. Come into our spirits. We invite you in. Now. Lord. Amen.

CHAPTER 9
THE GOOD SAMARITAN

Prayer:

Show us the way You want us to go and give us the wisdom to follow Your lead. We pray in Jesus' name. Amen.

Kitty Genovese

On March 13, 1964, at about 2:30 a.m., twenty-eight-year-old Catherine Susan "Kitty" Genovese, a vivacious bar manager for Ev's Eleventh Hour Bar, left work, got into her red Fiat, and headed to her apartment in a nice middle-class area of Queens, NY. She was the oldest of five children of an Italian American family. Her father owned a coat and apron supply business. She was ambitious. She was working double shifts hoping to save enough money to open an Italian restaurant.

At a red light, she was spotted by a 29-year-old stranger named Winston Mosely, who was parked. He followed her home. She parked her car in a parking lot that was 100 feet from her second-floor apartment. She turned off the lights and began walking. She was near a streetlight when Moseley grabbed her from behind and stabbed her twice in the back. She screamed.

Lights went on. Windows opened in the 10-floor apartment building nearby. She yelled, "Oh, my God, he stabbed me! Please help me!" A man's voice shouted, "Let that girl alone. "The attacker was surprised. He looked up, shrugged and walked-off down the street. Kitty Genovese struggled to get to her feet. Lights went back off. Windows closed in the apartments. Nobody did anything.

Moseley came back. He stabbed her again. She cried out, "I'm dying! I'm dying!" Again, the lights came on and again the windows opened in many of the nearby apartments and again the man left. This time he got into his car and drove away for about 10 minutes.

Kitty Genovese staggered to her feet as a city bus drove by. It was now 3:35 a.m. Again, the lights were turned off, and again the windows were shut. Again, her attacker returned. He found her in the doorway of her apartment at the foot of the stairs. He resumed his attack, raped her, and wound up stabbing her a total of 14 times. He stole $49 from her. One news account, that has since been questioned, reported that thirty-eight people saw or heard what was going on.

The police received the first call at 3:50 a.m. They were at the scene within two minutes, but Kitty Genovese was already dead. When people were interviewed during the investigation, several responded, "I didn't want to get involved." Others said, "I thought it was a domestic dispute."

Kitty Genovese's death helped inspire the creation of 911.

James 4:17 (KJV) "Therefore, to him that knoweth to do good, and doeth it not, to him it is sin."

James 4:17 (LNT) "Remember, too, that knowing what is right to do and then not doing it is sin."

James 4:17 (RSV) "Whoever knows what is right to do and fails to do it, for him it is sin."

What keeps us from doing the good that we should be doing?

Many times, during the 59 years I have practiced law, particularly in child custody cases when people know things that would help keep a child out of a bad environment, they tell me, "I don't want to get involved!"

Why are we like that?

Lawyer

Speaking of lawyers, one day a lawyer decided to test Jesus.

Luke 10:25-28 (LNT) "One day an expert on Moses' laws came to test Jesus' orthodoxy by asking Him this question: 'Teacher, what does a man need to do to live forever in heaven?' 26 Jesus replied, 'What does Moses' law say about it?' 27 'It says,' he replied, 'that you must love the Lord your God with all your heart, and with all your soul, and with all your strength, and with all your mind. And you must love your neighbor just as much as you love yourself.' 28 'Right!' Jesus told him. 'Do this and you shall live!'"

We talked a little about this last week, remember? We learned that God not only forgives sin, but He even forgets it.

Hebrews 8:12 (KJV) "For I will be merciful to their unrighteousness, and their sins and their iniquities will I remember no more."

Psalm 103:12 (KJV) "As far as the east is from the west, so far hath he removed our transgressions from us."

Isaiah 43:25 (NIV) "I, even I, am he who blots out your transgressions, for my own sake, and remembers your sins no more."

Last week we struggled with the criteria God uses to judge us if he forgives and forgets our sins. Remember Jesus told the lawyer that he was right that we must love our neighbor just as much as we love ourselves. But the lawyer asked Jesus another question.

Luke 10:29 (RSV) "But he, desiring to justify himself, said to Jesus, 'And who is my neighbor?'"

How would we answer that question today? "Who is our neighbor?"

Parable of The Good Samaritan

Jesus responded to the question with a parable.

Luke 10:30-37 (RSV) "Jesus replied, 'A man was going down from Jerusalem to Jericho, and he fell among robbers, who stripped him and beat him, and departed, leaving him half dead. 31 Now by chance a priest was going down that road; and when he saw him, he passed by on the other side. 32 So likewise a Levite, when he came to the place and saw him, passed by on the other side. 33 But a Samaritan, as he journeyed, came to where he was; and when he saw him, he had compassion, 34 and went to him and bound up his wounds, pouring on oil and wine; then he set him on his own beast and brought him to an inn, and took care of him. 35 And the next day he took out two denarii and gave them to the innkeeper, saying, 'Take care of him; and whatever more you spend, I will repay you when I come back.' 36 Which of these three do you think proved neighbor to the man who fell among the robbers?' 37 He said, 'The one who showed mercy on him.' And Jesus said to him, 'Go and do likewise.'"

Let me set the scene for you. Jerusalem is 2,300 feet above sea level. The Dead Sea, which is near Jericho, is 1,300 feet below sea level. In the space of less than 20 miles, the road drops some 3,600 feet. It has narrow, rocky passages and sudden turns which lend themselves to hiding places for thieves. For centuries people avoided going down that road alone. They normally went in caravans figuring safety in numbers. So, the foolhardy man who attempted to go down that road alone, got what would have been predicted. It is hard to feel sorry for someone who was so reckless. He had nobody to blame but himself.

The priest might have been on his way to church. He may have thought the man were dead. If so, and he touched him, he would be unclean and unable to participate in any temple activities for a week.

Number 19:11 (KJV) "He that toucheth the dead body of any man shall be unclean seven days."

Number 19:13 (LB) "Anyone who touches a dead person and does not purify himself in the manner specified, has defiled the Tabernacle of the Lord, and shall be excommunicated from Israel."

Numbers 19:17 (LB) "To become purified again, ashes from the red heifer sin offering are to be added to spring water in a kettle. 18 Then a person who is not defiled shall take hyssop branches and dip them into the water and sprinkle the water upon the tent and upon all the pots and pans in the tent, and upon anyone who has been defiled by being in the tent, or by touching a bone, or touching someone has been killed or is otherwise dead, or has touched a grave. 19 This shall take place on the third and seventh days; then the defiled person must wash his clothes and bathe himself, and that evening he will be out from under the defilement."

Now if this happened to be during the Feast of the Passover, priests had to wait as long as three years to earn the right to participate in temple activities at that time. If the priest touched a dead person, his three-year wait would be for naught.

The Levite? He was probably on his way to church as well. He may have had the same excuse as the priest, but he also may have remembered that a common trick of thieves was to dummy up one of their own to look like he had been beaten. When some kind soul stopped to see if he could help, the thieves would jump him.

A Samaritan? Samaritans were despised by the Jews. Samaritans were not allowed to worship at the Temple in Jerusalem. They were not allowed to marry a Jew. Samaritans were not permitted to participate in the rebuilding of the Temple. They were not allowed to buy large cattle. As a result of a three-year struggle with Syria in 722-721 B.C., 27,290 Samaritans were taken into captivity and replaced with Syrians. Thousands of peasants were left behind ultimately resulting in a racially mixed population of Samaria.

2 Kings 17:23-28 (LB) "...until the Lord finally swept them away, just as all his prophets had warned would happen. So, Israel was carried off to the land of Assyria where they remain to this day. 24 And the king of Assyria transported colonies of people from Babylon, Cuthah, Avva, Hamath, and Sepharvaim and resettled them in the cities of Samaria, replacing the people of Israel. So, the Assyrians took over Samaria and the other cities of Israel. 25 But since these Assyrian colonists did not worship the Lord when they first arrived, the Lord sent lions among them to kill some of them. 26 Then they sent a message to the king of Assyria: 'We colonists here in Israel don't know the laws of the god of the land, and he has sent lions among us to destroy us because we have not worshiped him.' 27-28 The king of Assyria then decreed that one of the exiled priests from Samaria should return to Israel and teach the new residents the laws of the god of the land. So, one of them returned to Bethel and taught the colonists from Babylon how to worship the Lord."

Thus, the Jews looked down their noses at the Samaritans because they had intermarried with the Assyrians and were not pure Jews, but a mixed breed. Jews normally would not even speak to a Samaritan. Further, Samaritans based their faith on the first five books of the Bible, called the Pentateuch.

John 4:7-9 (LNT) "Soon a Samaritan woman came to draw water, and Jesus asked her for a drink. 8 He was alone at the time as His disciples had gone into the village to buy some food. 9 The woman was surprised that a Jew would ask a 'despised Samaritan' for anything— usually they won't even speak to them–and she remarked about this to Jesus."

So, when Jesus spoke to the woman at the well, she was surprised. Even Jesus disliked the Samaritans. When instructing his disciples in spreading the Gospel, he gave them the following instructions:

Matthew 10:5-7 (LNT) "Jesus sent them out with these instructions: 'Don't go to the Gentiles or the Samaritans, 6 But only to the people of Israel–God's lost sheep. 7 Go and announce to them that the Kingdom of Heaven is near.'"

Are we sometimes like the Priest and the Levite? How?

What should we be doing in cases such as Kitty Genovese and the victim The Good Samaritan helped?

One of the members of our Sunday School Class says that she keeps bottles of water and energy bars in her car and hands them out to people who are homeless or have signs saying, "I will work for food" or "Please help."

How often do we pass by on the other side of the road?

Do we sometimes just miss the point of our faith?

Does Christianity at times simply become just a religion to us and not a lifestyle?

Internet Posting

My wife, Judy, showed me a posting on the Internet. A lady went into a restaurant, ordered food, and found that she did not have enough money to pay for it. She went around the restaurant asking people to help her pay for her food. A young black boy took her by the arm and said, "I got this."

He took her back to the counter, paid for her food and left. He did not care about her color or the fact that she ordered the food when she probably knew she could not pay for it. He simply saw a person in need and decided to do something about it. A woman ran after him and asked him his name. She told him that he had made that woman's day as well as her own for the example he set.

Jesus would have told us: "Go and do thou likewise."

How do we do this?

By giving money? By taking the person begging to a restaurant and paying for his food? By carrying bottles of water and energy bars in our vehicles and handing them out to people in need?

Prayer:

Lord, you have told us to love our neighbor as much as we love ourselves. Guide us, Lord, that we might obey your command and live, as You promised. We pray in Jesus' name. Amen.

CHAPTER 10
DANIEL

Prayer:

Lord, this morning we would open ourselves to You and ask that you direct our lives in the way You want us to go. We pray in Jesus' name. Amen.

Daniel, who was one of the major prophets, was born in 621 B.C. to a noble Judean family. To put Daniel in perspective, that would be 100 years after the Syrians conquered Samaria and in 722 and 721 B.C. and replaced 27,290 of them with Syrians as we learned last week. The Syrians and the Samaritans intermarried. Remember that caused the Jews to look down on Samaritans because they were of mixed blood and not pure Jews.

The name, "Daniel," means "God is my judge." He inspired later generations to be faithful to God's law in times of trial by showing that faithfulness could bring success even under very adverse circumstances.

Hostages

Daniel was one of four best and brightest youthful hostages taken to Babylon by King Nebuchadnezzar when he was 16 in 605 B.C. For three years Daniel and his friends were trained to read and write Aramaic and learned scientific and diplomatic skills that allowed them to work effectively in the most powerful court of the Chaldeans. He was assigned the Babylonian name Belteshazzar, which means "protect his life." His friends were called Shadrach, Meshach, and Abednego. The four were official "wise men."

Daniel 1:6-7 (KJV) "Now among these were of the children of Judah, Daniel, Hananiah, Mishael and Azariah: 7 Unto whom the prince of the eunuchs gave names: for he gave unto Daniel the name of Belteshazzar; and to Hananiah, of Shadrach; and to Mishael, of Meshach; and to Azariah, of Abednego."

Daniel and his friends were permitted to eat the finest food in the land, the same food served to the King.

Daniel 1:5 (KJV) "And the king appointed them a daily provision of the king's meat, and of the wine which he drank."

Daniel declared that he would not defile himself by eating the King's food. He requested a vegetarian diet for himself and his friends. They wound up having a contest.

Daniel 1:15-16 (LB) "Well at the end of ten days, Daniel and his three friends looked healthier and better nourished than the youths who had been eating the food supplied by the king! 16 So after that the steward fed them only vegetables and water, without the rich foods and wine."

Daniel 1:15-16 (KJV) "And at the end of ten days their countenances appeared fairer and fatter in flesh than all the children which did eat the portion of the king's meat. 16 Thus Melzar took away the portion of their meat, and the wine that they should drink; and gave them pulse."

"Pulse" means vegetable foods, such as beans, lentils, and peas. After a 10- day experiment in which they actually gained weight, they were permitted to have a vegetarian diet. Daniel demonstrated that faithfulness in God was a better way of life.

Daniel 1:17 (KJV) "As for these four children, God gave them knowledge and skill in all learning and wisdom: and Daniel had understanding in all visions and dreams."

Daniel 1:20 (KJV) "And in all matters of wisdom and understanding, that the king inquired of them, he found them ten times better than all the magicians and astrologers that were in all his realm."

King's Dream

God bestowed upon Daniel the gift of visions and of interpreting dreams. He enjoyed high honors. King Nebuchadnezzar had a dream which none of his magicians or sorcerer were able to guess what it was. They asked him to tell them about the dream, but he was not able to remember it.

The magicians and sorcerers approached the king and said:

Daniel 2:4-6 (KJV) "O king, live forever: tell thy servants the dream, and we will shew the interpretation. 5 The king answered and said to the Chaldeans, The thing is gone from me: if ye will not make known unto me the dream, with the interpretation thereof, ye shall be cut in pieces, and your houses shall be made a dunghill. 6 But if ye shew the dream, and the interpretation thereof, ye shall receive of me gifts and rewards and great honour: therefore shew me the dream, and the interpretation thereof."

Death Sentence

He gave all of the wise men, including Daniel and his friends, a death sentence.

Daniel 2:13 (KJV) "And the decree went forth that the wise men should be slain; and they sought Daniel and his fellows to be slain."

Daniel 2:16 (LB) "So, Daniel went in to see the king. 'Give me a little time,' he said, 'and I will tell you the dream and what it means.'"

Daniel 2:19 (LB) "And that night in a vision God told Daniel what the king had dreamed."

Interpretation of King's Dream

Daniel revealed to the King not only what the dream was but what it meant.

Daniel told the King that he had dreamed of a large statue. The head was of fine gold, its breast and arms were of silver, its belly and thighs of bronze and its legs of iron. Its feet were partly of iron and partly of clay. Suddenly a stone untouched by human hands strikes the image and broke it into dust that the wind scattered while the stone grew into a mountain.

Daniel told him that he was the head of gold in the dream. However, his dynasty would not last. He would be replaced by lesser kingdoms which were represented by the silver and bronze. Those would in turn be broken by the iron which turned out to be the Greeks led by Alexander the Great, representing God whose kingdom would last forever.

King Nebuchadnezzar was so astonished at Daniel's interpretation that he confessed the God of the Jews was the "God of gods and Lord of kings."

Daniel 2:46 (KJV) "Then the king Nebuchadnezzar fell upon his face, and worshiped Daniel, and commanded that they should offer an oblation and sweet odours unto him."

"Oblation" means an offering–a nonliving sacrifice. "Odours" or "odors" is a pleasant or sweet smell. Probably an incense.

The king placed Daniel over all Babylonian wise men and made him governor over the entire province of Babylon itself. Daniel transferred this appointment to his three friends.

Daniel 2:48-49 (LB) "Then the king made Daniel very great; he gave him many costly gifts; and appointed him to be ruler over the whole province of Babylon, as well as chief over all his wise men. 49 Then, at Daniel's request, the king appointed Shadrach, Meshach, and Abednego as Daniel's assistants, to be in charge of all the affairs of the province of Babylon; Daniel served as chief magistrate in the king's court."

King's Later Life

Later in his life King Nebuchadnezzar became a raging tyrant and demanded idol worship and burned to death those who would not comply. He erected a huge golden statue and assembled all the high officials and commanded them to prostrate themselves before it at the sound of the horn, bagpipe, harp or any sound of music.

Shadrach, Meshach and Abednego refused to bow down to the graven image. The king gave them a second chance, but they replied:

Daniel 3:16-18 (LB) "Shadrach, Meshach, and Abednego replied, 'O Nebuchadnezzar, we are not worried about what will happen to us. 17 If we are thrown into the flaming furnace, our God is able to deliver us; and he will deliver us out of your hand, Your Majesty. 18 But if he doesn't, please understand, sir, that even then we will never under any circumstances serve your gods or worship the golden statute you have erected.'"

The king had them bound and thrown into a fiery or blazing furnace when they refused to comply. He heated the fire to seven times "hotter than usual." The heat was so great that the servants who threw them in burned to death in the process. God sent an angel into the furnace to protect them, and they survived. The King commanded them to come out. Not a hair on their heads was singed, their clothing was not harmed, and they did not even smell of smoke. That miracle converted King Nebuchadnezzar once again to the God of the Jews. He even threatened death to anyone who spoke against God.

Other Dreams

In the later years of King Nebuchadnezzar's reign, Daniel interpreted the King's dream of the fallen tree. The tree reached into the sky. It provided abundant fruit. Birds nested in its branches. Animals took shelter beneath it. A holy one came down from Heaven and cut down the tree leaving only a stump in the ground.

The King had fallen away from God. Daniel said that the tree represented the King and predicted that the King would be humbled by becoming as a beast for seven years. Daniel begged the King to repent and change his ways, but he did not. A year later the prophecy came true. The King was rebuked by a voice from Heaven. He became mad, went around on all fours, and ate grass like an animal. When he was restored to his senses seven years later, he had his entire country adopt Jehovah as their God.

King Nebuchadnezzar's son, Belshazzar, took over when the King retired. Daniel interpreted the dream of the four great beasts and later the dream of the ram and the he-goat.

King Belshazzar was guilty of profane revelries. During one of his big feasts which featured thousands of guests, he and his guests drank wine out of holy temple vessels. During the party, a man's hand appeared and began writing on the wall with his finger.

Daniel 5:24-25 (LB) "And so, God sent those fingers to write this message: 'Mene,' Mene,', Tekel,' "Parsin.'"

King Belshazzar was terrified and summoned Daniel. Daniel interpreted the writing as follows:

Daniel 5:26-28 (LB):

Mene (meanie)--"God has numbered the days of your kingdom and brought it to an end."

Tekel (tee-kell) --"You have been weighed in the balances and found wanting."

Peres (pee-rez) the singular of Parsin (parson)--"Your kingdom is divided and given to the Medes and Persians."

Daniel thus interpreted the writing by predicting a Medo-Persian victory over Belshazzar, which happened that very night and Belshazzar was killed

Darius the Mede took over and made Daniel, who was then about 80 years old, one of his three presidents who would direct 120 governors who ruled the empire for the King. King Darius was considering him for the post of chief administrator. Daniel's colleagues were jealous. They were not able to find any evidence of corruption against Daniel. They contrived against him by flattering Darius into signing a royal edict which could not be broken or changed saying that all prayers will be only to Darius for 30 days on pain of being thrown into the lions' den if disobeyed. Daniel continued worshiping God three times a day before an open window facing Jerusalem.

His rivals brought charges against him. He was arrested and taken before a reluctant Darius, who had no choice because of the unchangeable law but to condemn Daniel to be thrown into the lions' den. He was. However, God protected him. The next morning a sleepless, fasting, and worried King Darius was overjoyed to find Daniel unharmed.

Daniel 6:21-22 (RSV) "Then Daniel said to the king, 'O king, live forever. 22 My God sent his angel and shut the lions' mouths and they have not hurt me, because I was found blameless before him; and also, before you, O king, I have done no wrong.'"

King Darius then threw Daniel's accusers into the lions' den, and they were immediately killed.

Daniel 6:26 (RSV) He issued an edict commanding all to "fear before the God of Daniel, for He is the living God, enduring forever."

Daniel's last prophecies were an overpowering vision of future events involving the persecution of the Jews and the archangel Michael contending with the demonic powers of a pagan society.

Daniel was not privileged to live to see these prophecies fulfilled. He also predicted the coming of the Messiah.

What are your thoughts about what we can learn about Daniel?

Grandmother

Two young boys were talking one afternoon. One said, "My Grandmother always has something nice to say about everybody." The second boy said he wanted to challenge the grandmother. They went to her. The second boy said to her, "I hear you always have something nice to say about everybody." She thought for a moment, and then agreed that this was true.

"What can you say good about the Devil?" the boy asked.

She thought a minute and then said, "Well, he's a hard worker."

Conclusion

Probably today the Devil is working harder than ever before to mislead us. We need to stay the course as did Daniel and his friends. More than ever before, we need to share our faith with others so that Christianity can spread.

Our final thought for the day. When the hand comes to write on the wall about each one of us, will it write, "You have been weighed in the balances and found wanting?"

Or will it write:

"Well done thy good and faithful servant?"

Prayer.

Lord, our prayer today is for you to guide us so that we may never be found wanting in your eyes. We ask this in Your Son's name. Amen.

CHAPTER 11
THE TEN COMMANDMENTS, PART 1

Prayer:

Lord, this morning we ask that you teach us Your way. We pray in Jesus' name. Amen.

The Struggle

The time is 1491 B.C. or 1491 years before Christ was born. Moses would ultimately become the most important prophet in Judaism and an important prophet in Christianity and other religions. The first five books of the Bible, called the "Torah" or the "Pentateuch" were probably written by him. Moses was not only a great leader for the people of Israel but also their lawgiver.

God had asked Moses to lead the Israelites out of Egypt. His response?

Exodus 4:10 (NIV) "Moses said to the Lord, 'O Lord, I have never been eloquent, neither in the past nor since you have spoken to your servant. I am slow of speech and tongue."

Exodus 4:10 (LB) "But Moses pleaded, 'O Lord, I'm just not a good speaker. I never have been, and I'm not now, even after you have spoken to me, for I have a speech impediment.'"

God said:

Exodus 4:12 (NIV) "Now go; I will help you speak and will teach you what to say."

Moses replied:

Exodus 4:13 (NIV) "O Lord, please send someone else to do it."

Have things changed in the last 3,500 years?

When God calls, do we immediately respond in a positive fashion?

What excuses do we use today to avoid God's calling?

After Moses offered excuses, God asked Moses to consider getting help from his brother, Aaron.

Exodus 4:14-16 (NIV) "Then the Lord's anger burned against Moses, and he said, 'What about your brother, Aaron the Levite? I know he can speak well. 15 You shall speak to him and put words in his mouth; I will help both of you speak and will teach you what to do. 16 He will speak to the people for you, and it will be as if he were your mouth and as if you were God to him.'"

So, Moses and his big brother, Aaron, who was three years older, became a team. They served the one true God known as Jehovah, Yahweh, El Shaddai or Adonai.

Plagues

Exodus 5:1 (NIV) "Afterward Moses and Aaron went to Pharaoh and said, 'This is what the Lord, the God of Israel, says: 'Let my people go, so that they may hold a festival to me in the desert.'"

Let's hear Pharaoh's response:

Exodus 5:2 (NIV) "Pharaoh said, 'Who is the Lord, that I should obey him and let Israel go? I do not know the Lord and I will not let Israel go.'"

The first plague was to turn the Nile River into blood. That caused all the fish in the river to die. Pharaoh was unfazed. The second plague was frogs.

Exodus 8:8 (NIV) "Pharaoh summoned Moses and Aaron and said, 'Pray to the Lord to take the frogs away from me and my people, and I will let your people go to offer sacrifices to the Lord.'"

Moses cried out to the Lord, and the frogs died. Pharaoh changed his mind.

Next Moses stretched out his hand and the third plague was that of gnats. Pharaoh remained unconvinced.

Then the Lord sent swarms of flies. The land was ruined.

Exodus 8:28 (NIV) "Pharaoh said, 'I will let you go to offer sacrifices to the Lord your God in the desert, but you must not go very far. Now pray for me.'"

Moses took the flies away. Pharaoh's heart hardened again. He refused to let the Israelites go.

The fifth plague saw all of the Egyptians' animals die including horses, donkeys, camels, cattle, sheep and goats. Pharaoh still refused to let the people of Israel go.

Next Moses tossed a handful of soot from a furnace in the presence of Pharaoh and boils broke out on men and animals. Pharaoh still did not listen.

Hail was a rare event for Egypt. Moses said to Pharaoh:

Exodus 9:18 (NIV) "Therefore, at this time tomorrow I will send the worst hailstorm that has ever fallen on Egypt from the day it was founded till now."

Moses stretched out his hand and the hail, the seventh plague, killed unprotected men.

Exodus 9:27-28 (NIV) "Then Pharaoh summoned Moses and Aaron. 'This time I have sinned,' he said to them. 'The Lord is in the right, and I and my people are in the wrong. 28 Pray to the Lord, for we have had enough thunder and hail. I will let you go; you don't have to stay any longer.'"

Deja vu. Moses stopped the hail. Pharaoh's heart hardened again. Pharaoh offered a compromise.

Exodus 10:10-11 (NIV) "Pharaoh said, 'The Lord be with you–if I let you go with your women and children! Clearly you are bent on evil. 11 No! Have only the men go; and worship the Lord since that's what you have been asking for."

We are talking about 600,000 men here. If you add women and children, the total of Israelites being held captive in Egypt was over two million. Moses stretched out his hand again, and Egypt was covered with locusts.

Exodus 10:16 (NIV) "Pharaoh quickly summoned Moses and Aaron and said, 'I have sinned against the Lord your God and against you. 17 Now forgive my sin once more and pray to the Lord your God to take this deadly plague away from me.'"

After all the locusts were gone, Pharaoh changed his mind–again–and would not let the Israelites go.

The ninth plague was darkness. The Israelites had light. No one else could see for three days.

Pharaoh tried to bargain again.

Exodus 10:24 (NIV) "Then Pharaoh summoned Moses and said, 'Go, worship the Lord. Even your women and children may go with you; only leave your flocks and herds behind.'"

No deal. Moses remained firm. The tenth and final plague was death. Moses instructed the Israelites to put the blood of a lamb or a goat on the top and sides of their door frames. Then God told Moses

Exodus 12:12-13 (NIV) "On that same night I will pass through Egypt and strike down every firstborn–both men and animals–and I will bring judgment on all the gods of Egypt. I am the Lord. The blood will be a sign for you on the houses where you are; and when I see the blood, I will pass over you. No destructive plague will touch you when I strike Egypt."

Exodus 12:29 (NIV) "At midnight the Lord struck down all the firstborn in Egypt, from the firstborn of Pharaoh, who sat on the throne, to the firstborn of the prisoner, who was in the dungeon, and the firstborn of all the livestock as well."

Exodus 12:31-32 (NIV) "During the night Pharaoh summoned Moses and Aaron and said, 'Up! Leave my people you and the Israelites! Go, worship the Lord as you have requested. Take your flocks and herds, as you have said and go. And also bless me.'"

Losing his son brought Pharaoh to his knees. The Egyptian people were most anxious for the Israelites to leave.

Exodus 12:33 (NIV) "The Egyptians urged the people to hurry and leave the country. 'For otherwise,' they said, 'we will all die.'"

The Israelites left so quickly that they carried their dough with them in kneading troughs before yeast was added. Further, they took advantage of the frightened Egyptians. It was going to take a lot of money and provisions to feed and clothe two million people.

Exodus 12:35-36 (NIV) "The Israelites did as Moses instructed and asked the Egyptians for articles of silver and gold and for clothing. The Lord had made the Egyptians favorably disposed toward the people and they gave them what they asked for; so, they plundered the Egyptians."

What impact did the sudden leaving of two million Israelites have on Egypt?

Maybe the wealthy Egyptians had nobody to mow their lawns. Maybe the wealthy Egyptians had nobody to nanny their children. Maybe the wealthy Egyptians had forgotten how to cook for themselves. Maybe suddenly subtracting two million people from the local economy caused a depression. Whatever, Pharaoh changed his mind, again.

Exodus 14:5 (NIV) "What have we done? We have let the Israelites go and have lost their services!"

Pharaoh took his army with him and set out to bring the Israelites back.

God led the people of Israel.

Exodus 13:22 (NIV) "Neither the pillar of cloud by day nor the pillar of fire by night left its place in front of the people."

When the Israelites saw the Egyptians coming after them, they lost faith in Moses. They were terrified. "It is better to serve the Egyptians than die in the desert," they said.

God set a trap for the Egyptians. He moved the cloud that was leading the Israelites from the front of them to the back. It was dark behind them. The Egyptians could not see. However, it was light in front of the Israelites.

Exodus 14:1-3 (NIV) "Then the Lord said to Moses, 'Tell the Israelites to turn back and encamp near Pi Hahiroth, between Migdol and the sea. They are to encamp by the sea, directly opposite Baal-Zephon. Pharaoh will think, 'The Israelites are wandering around the land in confusion, hemmed in by the desert.'"

The Egyptian army caught up with the Israelites that night.

Exodus 14:21-22 (NIV) "Then Moses stretched out his hand over the sea, and all that night the Lord drove the sea back with a strong east wind and turned it into dry land. The waters were divided, and the Israelites went through the sea on dry ground, with a wall of water on their right and on their left."

More than 600 chariots and thousands of soldiers followed the Israelites into the sea. Can you picture this? The Egyptian soldiers are in hot pursuit. The best trained army in the world charges into an ambush. Couldn't they see the sea on the right that the sea on their left, standing there like a wall? After witnessing the 10 plagues, wouldn't they be at least a little cautious to challenge the God of the Israelites? They obviously thought that rounding up the 600,000 men with their wives and children would be a walk in the park. Like many people before and many people after, they underestimated God's ability to assist those He chooses.

Exodus 14:26-28 (NIV) "Then the Lord said to Moses, 'Stretch out your hand over the sea so that the waters may flow back over the Egyptians and their chariots and horsemen.' 27 Moses stretched out his hand over the sea, and at daybreak the sea went back to its place. The Egyptians were fleeing toward it, and the Lord swept them into the sea. 28 The water flowed back and covered the chariots and horsemen–the entire army of Pharaoh that had followed the Israelites into the sea. Not one of them survived."

What reaction do you think the people of Israel had when they saw this happening?

Exodus 14:31 (NIV) "And when the Israelites saw the great power the Lord displayed against the Egyptians, the people feared the Lord and put their trust in Him and in Moses His servant."

Exodus tells us that not one of the Egyptians survived. That causes me to believe that Pharaoh was killed in the Red Sea with his soldiers. However, critics point out that the Bible does not say that Pharaoh was killed. When a king is killed, it is a big deal. There would probably be mention of it somewhere in history.

There are two theories among people who do not think Pharaoh died in the Red Sea. One is that he continued as Pharaoh and ruled Egypt 22 years. The other is that he moved to Nineveh and became the king there. They believe that he was the king at the time when Jonah made his prediction that in 40 days they would be wiped out. They say that he recognized the power of the Lord and let the people of Nineveh live by personally putting on sackcloth and ashes to demonstrate repentance.

Before reaching Mount Sinai, the Israelites had to fight off the Amalekites, but the Lord helped them defeat the Amalekites.

Father-in-Law

Exodus 18:2 (NIV) "After Moses had sent away his wife Zipporah, his father-in-law Jethro received her and her two sons."

I see Moses doing this as a precaution. If the Egyptians had caught them or if the Amalekites had won the battle, Moses' wife and children would probably have been in great danger.

Exodus 18:9 (NIV) "Jethro was delighted to hear about all the good things the Lord had done for Israel in rescuing then from the hand of the Egyptians."

After giving Moses some good advice about delegating authority, Jethro left Zipporah and her children there and returned to his own country.

Mount Sinai

The Israelites were in bondage in Egypt for 430 years.

Exodus 12:40 (NIV) "Now the length of time the Israelite people lived in Egypt was 430 years. At the end of the 430 years, to the very day, all the Lord's divisions left Egypt."

It took the Israelites exactly three months to reach the base of Mount Sinai.

Exodus 19:1 (NIV) "In the third month after the Israelites left Egypt–on the very day–they came to the Desert of Sinai."

They camped there for 11 months and five days. They were probably camped at the foot of the mountain where there is a 2½ by ½ mile peninsula. Moses was prepared to climb Mount Sinai and receive the Ten Commandments from the Lord.

There are two mountains that authorities are divided over which one was the one Moses climbed. Mount Catherine is 8,625 feet high. Jebel Musa is 7,497 feet high. Most of the authorities favor Jebel Musa.

The Lord required three things of the Israelites before He gave then the Ten Commandments.

Exodus 19:10-12 (NIV) "And the Lord said to Moses, 'Go to the people and consecrate them today and tomorrow. Have them wash their clothes 11 and be ready by the third day, because on that day the Lord will come down on Mount Sinai in the sight of all the people. 12 Put limits for the people around the mountain and tell them, 'Be careful that you do not go up the mountain or touch the foot of it. Whoever touches the mountain shall surely be put to death.'"

Exodus 19:14-15 (NIV) "After Moses had gone down the mountain to the people, he consecrated them, and they washed their clothes. 15 Then he said to the people, 'Prepare yourselves for the third day. Abstain from sexual relations.'"

So, Moses had the people wash their clothes, stay away from the mountain, and abstain from sex.

Exodus 19:16 (NIV) "On the morning of the third day there was thunder and lightning, with a thick cloud over the mountain, and a very loud trumpet blast. Everyone in the camp trembled."

Exodus 19:18-19 (NIV) "Mount Sinai was covered with smoke, because the Lord descended on it in fire. The smoke billowed up from it like smoke from a furnace, the whole mountain trembled violently, 19 and the sound of the trumpet grew louder and louder. Then Moses spoke and the voice of God answered him."

Do you think God, maybe, had the Israelites' attention?

When I heard about the smoke and fire, I immediately thought of a volcano erupting. There are no volcanos in the Sinai area. This was God speaking directly to the people of Israel.

Moses ascended the mountain and came back with two tablets. The first four Commandments were on the first tablet and the last six were on the second. There were two positive Commandments and eight negative Commandments.

The tablets were known as "The Ten Commandments," or "The Ten Words," or "The Decalogue."

Many people, in modern days, simple consider them, "The Ten Suggestions."

Which Commandments do we pay the least attention to?

Where do you think the expression "etched in stone" came from? What does it mean?

If it is etched in stone, does it mean that it can be changed?

In my profession as a lawyer, if an offer is "etched in stone," it means that this is the final offer. It will not be changed.

Psalm 19:7 (NIV) "The law of the Lord is perfect, reviving the soul. The statutes of the Lord are trustworthy, making the wise the simple."

Does God's Word sometimes seem too heavy?

Are God's laws perfect?

The receiving of the Ten Commandments was the first time in the Bible that God spoke directly to the people of Israel.

Why do you think He went to such lengths to impress upon them the importance of receiving the Ten Commandments?

In the next few lessons, we will be studying The Ten Commandments. In the meantime, think about this scripture:

James 1:22 (NIV) "Do not merely listen to the word, and so deceive yourselves, do what it says."

Prayer:

Lord, when you speak, help us to listen and put Your Words into our actions. We pray in your Son's Holy name. Amen.

CHAPTER 12
THE TEN COMMANDMENTS, PART 2

Prayer:

Lord, this morning we thank You for commandments on how to live. We pray for wisdom and understanding. In Jesus' name. Amen.

Do you believe that God punishes you for the sins of your grandfathers and great grandfathers?

What is an echo? (The same words coming back to us. Words that are repeated.)

Have one reader read Exodus 20:1-3 followed by someone who reads Deuteronomy 5:6-7. Then the first reader reads Exodus 20:4-6. The second reader reads Deuteronomy 5:8-10. The first reader reads Exodus 20:7. The second reader reads Deuteronomy 5:11. Then the first reader reads Exodus 20:7 and the second reads responds with Deuteronomy 5:11.

Exodus 20:1-7 (NIV) "And God spoke all these words: 2 'I am the Lord your God, who brought you out of Egypt, out of the land of slavery. 3 You shall have no other gods before me.

"4 You shall not make for yourself an idol in the form of anything in heaven above or on the earth beneath or in the waters below. 5 You shall not bow down to them or worship them: for I, the Lord your God, am a jealous god, punishing the children for the sin of the fathers to the third and fourth generation of those who hate me, 6 but showing love to a thousand generations of those who love me and keep my commandments. 7 You shall not misuse the name of the Lord your God, for the Lord will not hold anyone guiltless who misuses his name.'"

Deuteronomy 5:6-11 (NIV) "I am the Lord your God, who brought you out of Egypt, out of the land of slavery. 7 You shall have no other gods before me. 8 You shall not make for yourself an idol in the form of anything in heaven above or on the earth beneath or in the waters below. 9 You shall not bow down to them or worship them, for I the Lord your God, am a jealous God, punishing the children for the sin of the fathers to the third and fourth generation of those who hate me, 10 but showing love to a thousand generations of those who love me and keep my commandments. 11 You shall not misuse the name of the Lord your God, for the Lord will not hold anyone guiltless who misuses his name."

Did I hear an echo in here?

We learned last week that Moses delivered The Ten Commandments to the Israelites in 1491 B.C. Now here we are 40 years later in Deuteronomy in 1451 B. C. and Moses, like an echo, is giving The Ten Commandments to a different generation. Why would he do that?

Did you hear the first three Commandments?

They were identical. Word-for-word. Probably every man, woman and child had been required to memorize them during Moses' time. There is basically no difference in the Ten Commandments until you get to the Tenth Commandment.

Exodus 20:17 (NIV) "You shall not covet your neighbor's house. You shall not covet your neighbor's wife, or his manservant or maidservant, his ox or donkey, or anything that belongs to your neighbor."

Deuteronomy 5:21 (NIV) "You shall not covet your neighbor's wife. You shall not set your desire on your neighbor's house or land, his manservant or maidservant, his ox or donkey, or anything that belongs to your neighbor."

Did you catch the difference?

Years later, in Deuteronomy Moses adds to "your neighbor's house," "your neighbor's house or land!"

Wandering 40 Years in the Desert

Remember that the Israelites had wandered in the wilderness for 40 years. Instead of having faith in God when they neared the land of milk and honey, they had Moses send out 12 spies, one from each tribe. The spies came back with reports that the inhabitants of the Promised Land were giants and the cities had high walls. They refused to believe God would give them the land.

The generation of fighting men who refused to enter the Promised Land had died. The Israelites were without a home. They were without a place to put their heads down at night. It was 38 years after Moses went up and got the Ten Commandments, They were getting ready to become landowners in the land of milk and honey. Moses adds to what God originally said by saying not to set their desires on their neighbor's house OR LAND! Both the Living Bible and the New International Bible say OR LAND. The King James Version and the Revised Standard Version say, "OR FIELD."

Preface

As a preface to the First Commandment, God through Moses told the people of Israel:

"I AM the Lord, your God."

Or, put it this way:

"I am the Lord, YOUR God."

Why is this significant?

Does God require our loyalty today?

What do we put before God in today's world?

Is God a Person?

Is God a person?

Did Jesus look like His Father?

Genesis 1:26 (KJV) "And God said, 'Let us make man in our image, after our likeness.'"

Genesis 1:26 (LB) "And God said, 'Let us make a man–someone like ourselves.'"

Who is God talking about when he says, "Let US make a man in OUR image?"

God may not have a physical body, but does he think, act, love and have fellowship like a person?

A teacher said that a student in his Christian theology class surprised him in by saying that the student was offended when the teacher kept speaking of God as a person. He argued that saying God is a person diminishes God and brings Him down to our level. By doing this, the student said that God ceases to be God!

Do you agree?

A Description of God

God begins the Ten Commandments with a description of God: "I am the Lord your God, who brought you out of Egypt, out of the land of slavery."

Why is that significant?

Our lesson today suggests that God is love. He is explaining to the Israelites that he cared enough about them to bring them out of slavery and head them in the direction where they will have their own land–a land of milk and honey–which probably seems like it is too good to be true to these desert dwellers.

When something seems too good to be true, what is your first impression?

My sister spent over $6,000 upgrading her computer before she found out it was a hoax. It WAS too good to be true. My daughter paid a $7,000 deposit on an apartment in San Diego before realizing that the deal was too good to be true. Fortunately, she was able to stop payment on her check.

Let me ask you this: Does God's love for us seem too good to be true?

Finish this sentence for me, please: "God's love is like _____."

1 John 4:20 (NIV) "Whoever claims to love God yet hates a brother or sister is a liar. For whoever does not love their brother and sister, whom they have seen cannot love God, whom they have not seen."

Think about this: When God laid down the law in the Ten Commandments, he first talked about grace, how he brought the Israelites out of slavery. He put grace before the law.

Commands

The Israelites followed 613 commands. There were 248 positive commands, one for every part of the body. There were 365 negative commands, one for every day of the year. To them it was more important to follow the law than it was to be concerned about your neighbor.

Several years ago, a Methodist in White Deer, Texas, was badly injured in a vehicular collision in New Mexico on a weekend. On Sunday morning, there was no minister in the pulpit. He was in a New Mexico hospital with his church member. I was told that the church service that morning was one of the most meaningful the congregation had ever experienced.

Why do you think this was true?

Lawyer

You will remember that when the lawyer asked Jesus the loaded question about the greatest commandment and what Jesus' response was:

Matthew 22:36-38 (RSV) "'Teacher, which is the greatest commandment in the law?' 37 And he said to him, 'You shall love the Lord your God with all your heart and with all your soul and with all your mind. 38 This is the great and first commandment. 39 And a second is like it. You shall love your neighbor as yourself. 40 On these two commandments dependeth all the law and the prophets.'"

Shema

Deuteronomy 6:4-9 (NIV) "Hear, O Israel: The Lord our God, the Lord is one. 5 Love the Lord your God with all your heart and with all your soul and with all your strength. 6 These commandments that I give you today are to be upon your hearts. 7 Impress them on your children. Talk about them when you sit at home and when you walk along the road, when you lie down and when you get up. 8 Tie them as symbols on your hands and bind them on your foreheads. 9 Write them on the doorframes of your houses and on your gates."

The Israelites did exactly that! (Ask a member of the class to research and explain to the class about the Shema and a phylactery.)

Similes

Some say the Ten Commandments are so closely bound together that they are like a stringed instrument. A single broken string ruins the entire melody. The Ten Commandments are like the human body. If only one member is diseased, it may cause the death of the entire body. It is like a city with only one weakness or unguarded area. The enemy will enter at that weakness and subdue the entire city. I have heard it said, "Some of the people lost in hell kept a great many of the commandments; they are damned because they did not keep all of them."

Do we believe this?

Are these really Commandments or just suggestions?

The First Three Commandments

The first three commandments are Exodus 20:2-4 (KJV): "I am the Lord thy God, which have brought thee out of the land of Egypt, out of the house of bondage. Thou shalt have no gods before me. Thou shalt not make unto thee any graven image or any likeness of anything that is in heaven above, or that is in the earth beneath, or that is in the water under the earth."

The first three commandments show us our duty to God as our supreme Ruler, the Lord of our lives.

God, in the First Commandment, requires us to worship and be faithful to Him. He requires reverence in the Second Commandment and service in the Third.

Remember the concept of service?

Matthew 25:40 (NIV) The King will reply, 'I tell you the truth, whatever you did for one of the least of these brothers of mine, you did for me.'"

What does it mean to love God?

I think it means to be devoted to Him. Each of us needs to decide how to be devoted to Him. We demonstrate our love for God through service to others.

Back to the Ten Commandments. *What do you think about this scripture from James?*

James 2:10 (LB) "And the person who keeps every law of God, but makes one little slip, is just as guilty as the person who has broken every law there is."

James 2:10 (NIV) "For whoever keeps the whole law and yet stumbles at just one point is guilty of breaking all of it."

Last week we talked about whether God's laws are heavy.

Are these difficult laws to keep?

Why did Jesus say?

Matthew 11:30 (KJV and NIV) "For my yoke is easy, and my burden is light."

Fear God?

Deuteronomy 6:13 (NIV) "Fear the Lord your God serve him only."

Why should we be afraid of a kind, loving heavenly, perfect Father?

Questions

Should we question God?

Romans 9:20-21 (NIV) "But who are you, O man, to talk back to God? Shall what is formed say to him who formed it, 'Why did you make me like this?' Does not the potter have the right to make out of the same lump of clay some pottery for noble purposes and some for common use?'"

What do you think?

How do we sum up this lesson?

Sing Jesus Loves Me (or have a class member sing it).

Jesus loves me, this I know
For the Bible tells me so.
All of us to him belong.
We are weak, but he is strong.

Yes, Jesus loves me.
Yes, Jesus loves you.
Yes, Jesus loves us.

The Bible tells me so.

Prayer:

Let us pray. Lord, we realize that you love us. Help us to love each other the way you love us.

We pray in Jesus' name. Amen.

CHAPTER 13
THE TEN COMMANDMENTS, PART 3

Prayer:

Lord, Adonai, help us to listen to Your Word. Help us to understand. We pray in Jesus' name. Amen.

The Greek word for the Ten Commandments is "Decalogue," which means "Ten Words."

Exodus 20:3 (NIV) "You shall have no other gods before me."

What does "misplaced worship" mean?

What are examples?

Do we, at times, trivialize God's name today?

What are some examples of this?

I was the Democratic County Chair in Gray County for 10 years. I visited with a candidate for public office one day. He said, "God told me to run. He didn't promise me I would win, but He told me to run."

How do you feel about that?

Exodus 20:4 (LB) "You shall not make yourselves any idols, any images resembling animals, birds, or fish."

Romans 1:21-25 (NIV) "For although they knew God, they neither glorified him as God nor gave thanks to him, but their thinking became futile and their foolish hearts were darkened. 22 Although they claimed to be wise, they became fools 23 and exchanged the glory of the immortal God for images made to look like mortal man and birds and animals and reptiles. 24 Therefore God gave them over in the sinful desires of their hearts to sexual impurity for the degrading of their bodies with one another. 25 They exchanged the truth of God for a lie and worshiped and served created things rather than the Creator–who is forever praised. Amen."

Is the idolatry we are dealing with today more subtle than 3,500 years ago?

Is it more evil?

Are we more self-serving today than then?

Have we turned from God's ways to our own? (Calendars? Check books? Computers? Social Media?)

What are idols in our lives today?

Exodus 20:7 (NIV) "You shall not misuse the name of the Lord your God, for the Lord will not hold anyone guiltless who misuses his name."

How do we stay connected to God?

The Hebrew word, "godesh," is expressed primarily in the Old Testament by two images: purity and separation.

Hosea 11:9 (Last sentence, LB) "For I am God and not man; I am the Holy One living among you, and I did not come to destroy."

I took typing when I was a junior in high school. Dick sat next to me. One day he reached over to my desk, took my pencil, cracked it into two pieces on his desk and handed the pieces back to me with a sneer. I jumped up and slugged him.

Fortunately for me the teacher was not in the room at the time. "I'll see you after school," he snarled. After school, I saw him and asked him if he was still mad. He told me that he wanted to see me in a field between the high school and the Country Club.

Foolishly I went. When I got there, he was there with a half dozen of his friends. We squared off. I tried to box him, but I was surprised at how hard he could hit me. I changed tactics and tackled him. I got him down and forced open his right hand. In his hand was a pocketknife. No wonder he hit me so hard.

"Now that I have you down, I could do you dirty," I told him. "But I am not going to because I am a Christian." We were in the same Sunday School class. He never came back to Sunday School after that day.

Did I misuse or dishonor God's name?

Would a Christian have refused to fight him?

I had to go back to school to get a book I needed to do homework. I ran into my friend Rex. He looked at me and asked, "Did you have a fall?" "No," I said. "I've been in a fight." He laughed at me and said, "I know you better than that!"

The Fourth, Fifth and Sixth Commandments

Exodus 20:8 (NIV) "Remember the Sabbath day, by keeping it holy."

Exodus 20:12 (NIV) "Honor your father and your mother, so that you may live long in the land the Lord your God is giving you."

Exodus 20:13 (KJV) "Thou shalt not kill."

Exodus 20:13 (NIV) "You shall not murder."

Is there a difference in interpretation?

In war?

The hangman?

Self-defense?

To save the life of another?

To prevent a theft or felony?

I read about a man in Wichita Falls, Texas, who shot and killed a teenager who was stealing a watermelon.

Was that justified?

He was charged with manslaughter. The claim was that he used more force than was reasonably necessary.

What do you think?

The Seven and Eight Commandments

Exodus 20:14 (NIV) "You shall not commit adultery."

Exodus 20:15 (NIV) "You shall not steal

What if the bank teller makes a mistake when changing a $100 bill and gives you too much money?

An oil and gas man in Canadian, Texas went to see friends of his. They visited awhile. They invited him to supper. He accepted. They visited some more. As he was leaving, he quoted them a figure for their oil and gas rights which was extremely low. He knew it was, but they did not. Because they thought he was a friend and they trusted him, they took his offer.

Did he steal from them? Or is this just "business?"

The Ninth Commandment

Exodus 20:16 (NIV) "You shall not give false testimony against your neighbor."

Are we talking about perjury? Lying?

What about a white lie? How do you like my turnip and broccoli casserole? How do you like my dress? How do you like my hair cut?

Consider:

Teacher, "Johnny, did your daddy come home drunk again last night?" The truthful answer is, "Yes." Psychologists argue that it was none of the teacher's business to ask that question of Johnny and embarrass him before the entire class; he should say, "No." *Do you agree?*

Germans asked this question to Jehovah Witnesses in France in World War II. "Is this man a member of the underground?" If they said, "Yes" or if they refused to answer, he would be executed. If they said, "No," he would be released.

How should they answer that question?

The Tenth Commandment

Exodus 20:17 (NIV) "You shall not covet your neighbor's house. You shall not covet your neighbor's wife, or his manservant or maidservant, his ox or donkey or anything that belongs to your neighbor."

What is at the center of our lives today?

What do the Ten Commandments tell us about the character of God?

Are the Ten Commandments relevant today?

Summary

How do we sum up the Ten Commandments?

God in the First Commandment requires us to worship and be faithful to Him.

He requires reverence in the Second Commandment.

He requires service in the Third Commandment.

The Fourth contains our duty towards those who are God's representatives upon earth, and who are at the same time of all men our greatest benefactors.

The remaining six commandments contain our duties to ourselves and to our fellow-men:

The Fifth is for the protection of life, the Sixth of purity, the Seventh of property, the Eighth of honor, the Ninth and Tenth of the domestic life of one's neighbor.

Prayer:

God, reveal Yourself to us. Give us the insight to realize Your revelation. Give us the courage to reveal You to others. Amen.

CONCLUSION

I want to thank you for reading this book and I hope it has brought you closer to God and your own relationship with Him.

I have also created additional lessons and volumes to follow this. They are broken down to be able to jump in at any time and start a lesson plan.

If you would like to continue this journey, please look for Volume 2, 3 & 4 of this series. You can buy them individually or all together.

The eBook version can be downloaded into a tablet or ereader and the print version can be used by the group leader or by each person in the class.

If you have any questions or would like me to speak to your class virtually, I would love to be a guest speaker and hear how you like the book. You can email me here by clicking here: jww_pampa@yahoo.com

May God continue to bless you and your family as you help others get to know His word.

John W. Warner

About the Author

John W. Warner is a family man who has taught Sunday School classes in a small Texas town for over 50 years.

He is also an attorney who has been practicing for over 50 years. This book represents his love of God and his love of research.

About Defining Moments Press

Built for aspiring authors who are looking to share transformative ideas with others throughout the world, Defining Moments Press offers life coaches, healers, business professionals, and other non-fiction or self-help authors a comprehensive solution to getting their books published without breaking the bank or taking years.

Defining Moments Press prides itself on bringing readers and authors together to find tools and solutions.

As an alternative to self-publishing or signing with a major publishing house, we offer full profits to our authors, low-priced author copies, and simple contract terms.

Most authors get stuck trying to navigate the technical end of publishing. The comprehensive publishing services offered by Defining Moments Press mean that your book will be designed by an experienced graphic artist, available in printed, hard copy format, and coded for all eBook readers, including the Kindle, iPad, Nook, and more.

We handle all of the technical aspects of your book creation so you can spend more time focusing on your business that makes a difference for other people.

Defining Moments Press founder, publisher, and #1 bestselling author Melanie Warner has over 20 years of experience as a writer, publisher, master life coach, and accomplished entrepreneur.

You can learn more about Warner's innovative approach to self-publishing or take advantage of free trainings and education at: MyDefiningMoments.com.

Defining Moments Book Publishing

If you're like many authors, you have wanted to write a book for a long time, maybe you have even started a book...but somehow, as hard as you have tried to make your book a priority, other things keep getting in the way.

Some authors have fears about their ability to write or whether or not anyone will value what they write or buy their book. For others, the challenge is making the time to write their book or having accountability to finish it.

It's not just finding the time and confidence to write that is an obstacle. Most authors get overwhelmed with the logistics of finding an editor, finding a support team, hiring an experienced designer, and figuring out all the technicalities of writing, publishing, marketing, and launching a book. Others have actually written a book and might have even published it but did not find a way to make it profitable.

For more information on how to participate in our next Defining Moments Author Training program, visit: www.MyDefiningMoments.com. Or you can email Melanie@MyDefiningMoments.com.

Other #1 Bestselling Books by Defining Moments™ Press

Defining Moments: Coping With the Loss of a Child - Melanie Warner

Defining Moments SOS: Stories of Survival - Melanie Warner and Amber Torres

Write your Bestselling Book in 8 Weeks or Less and Make a Profit - Even if No One Has Ever Heard of You - Melanie Warner

Become Brilliant: Roadmap From Fear to Courage – Shiran Cohen

Unspoken: Body Language and Human Behavior For Business - Shiran Cohen

Rise, Fight, Love, Repeat: Ignite Your Morning Fire - Jeff Wickersham

Life Mapping: Decoding the Blueprint of Your Soul - Karen Loenser

Ravens and Rainbows: A Mother-Daughter Story of Grit, Courage and Love After Death – L. Grey and Vanessa Lynn

Pivot You! 6 Powerful Steps to Thriving During Uncertain Times – Suzanne R. Sibilla

A Workforce Inspired: Tools to Manage Negativity and Support a Toxic-Free Workplace – Dolores Neira

Journey of 1000 Miles: A Musher and His Huskies' Journey on the Century-Old Klondike Trails - Hank DeBruin and Tanya McCready

7 Unstoppable Starting Powers: Powerful Strategies For Unparalled Results From Your First Year as a New Leader – Olusegun Eleboda

Bouncing Back From Divorce With Vitality & Purpose: A Strategy For Dads – Nigel J Smart, PHD

Focus on Jesus and Not the Storm: God's Non-negotiables to Christians in America - Keith Kelley

Stepping Out, Moving Forward: Songs and Devotions - Jacqueline O'Neil Kelley

Time Out For Time In: How Reconnecting With Yourself Can Help You Bond With Your Child in a Busy Word - Jerry Le

The Sacred Art of Off Mat Yoga: Whisper of Wisdom Forever – Shakti Barnhill

The Beauty of Change: The Fun Way For Women to Turn Pain Into Power & Purpose – Jean Amor Ramoran

From No Time to Free Time: 6 Steps to Work/Life Balance For Business Owners - Christoph Nauer

Self-Healing For Sexual Abuse Survivors: Tired of Just Surviving, Time to Thrive - Nickie V. Smith

Prepared Bible Study Lessons: Weekly Plans For Church Leaders - John W. Warner

Frog on a Lily Pad - Michael Lehre

How to Effectively Supercharge Your Career as a CEO - Giorgio Pasqualin

Rising From Unsustainable: Replacing Automobiles and Rockets - J.P. Sweeney

Food - Life's Gift for Healing: Simple, Delicious & Life Saving Whole Food Plant Based Solutions - Angel and Terry Grier

Made in the USA
Las Vegas, NV
05 January 2025

15903478R00070